TINY TALKS

COME, FOLLOW ME

OTHER BOOKS BY HEIDI DOXEY

I Am Grateful for Colors
Jesus Was Just like Me
1, 2, 3 with Nephi and Me!
Time to Share: 52 Weeks of Primary Planning
Liam Darcy, I Loathe You

TINY TALKS SERIES
Tiny Talks: I Am a Child of God (2018)
Tiny Talks: Choose the Right (2017)
Tiny Talks: I Know My Savior Lives (2015)
Tiny Talks: Families Are Forever (2014)
Tiny Talks: I Am a Child of God (2013)
Tiny Talks: Choose the Right (2012)
Tiny Talks: I Know the Scriptures Are True (2011)

TINY
TALKS

COME, FOLLOW ME

HEIDI DOXEY

CFI
AN IMPRINT OF CEDAR FORT, INC.
SPRINGVILLE, UTAH

This is not an official publication of The Church of Jesus Christ of Latter-day Saints. The opinions and views expressed herein belong solely to the author and do not necessarily represent the opinions or views of Cedar Fort, Inc. Permission for the use of sources, graphics, and photos is also solely the responsibility of the author.

ISBN 13: 978-1-4621-2280-6

Published by CFI, an imprint of Cedar Fort, Inc.
2373 W. 700 S., Springville, UT 84663
Distributed by Cedar Fort, Inc., www.cedarfort.com

Library of Congress Control Number: 2018959494

Cover design by Shawnda T. Craig
Cover design © 2018 Cedar Fort, Inc.
Edited and typeset by Nicole Terry and Kaitlin Barwick

Printed in the United States of America

10 9 8 7 6 5 4 3 2 1

Printed on acid-free paper

Contents

CHAPTER 7: JULY

CHAPTER 8: AUGUST

CHAPTER 9: SEPTEMBER

CHAPTER 10: OCTOBER

CHAPTER 11: NOVEMBER

CHAPTER 12: DECEMBER

PRIMARY PROGRAM

ABOUT THE AUTHOR

Introduction

One of the most unique doctrines in our church is our belief that family relationships can be eternal. We are blessed with the knowledge that the people we love most can be with us forever. Because of this, we work hard to strengthen those relationships and create happy families where each member can learn and grow in the gospel. In this book we will focus on how our family relationships can become eternal through Heavenly Father's plan and the Savior's love and atoning sacrifice.

We will learn that Heavenly Father sent each of us to a family here on earth, that He has given us the tools and teachings we need to follow in order to create a happy family, and that He wants us to return to Him someday with all the members of our family—both those we know here on earth, and our ancestors who came before us. We realize that not every family situation is the same. With prayer and through the Spirit, you can be sensitive as you present the ideal of an eternal family while recognizing that some children may not currently be living that ideal. We know that through the Atonement, someday all things will be made right, and that no matter what our family situations are here on earth, if we remain faithful, we will be given every blessing promised to us, including the blessing of an eternal family.

I hope that throughout this year you will be prompted with specific things you can do to help your family and class members return to Heavenly Father. I also hope you will encourage the children you love to seek guidance from the Spirit as they learn these important doctrines. I am so grateful for my own family and for the reassuring knowledge I have that families can be forever.

HOW TO USE THIS BOOK

This book is designed to give you ideas for lessons, talks, scriptures, songs, and more. For each chapter, you will find an overview of resources that can be used throughout the month. Next you will find specific ideas for each week in the month, including talks and scriptures your children can give in Primary. Each week also includes a lesson and activity you can use in your home for family night or family scripture study, or as part of a lesson in a classroom setting.

Monthly Overview

MULTIMEDIA RESOURCES

The Church has created a wonderful library of videos and other content that can be accessed online. For each month, you'll find a suggested list of multimedia resources or online videos (with links) that you can use at any point throughout the month. Sometimes we learn better by having materials presented to us visually, so these videos can be a great way to engage children who might otherwise have a hard time paying attention. Before using one of these videos in your class, be sure to download it to your device or check to make sure you can stream it quickly at the church.

SONGS

Suggested songs are listed at the beginning of each month. These songs fit in with the Primary curriculum of "Come, Follow Me," as well as including some classic favorites that can be used all year. Unless otherwise specified, all songs are from the *Children's Songbook*.

GOSPEL ART BOOK

Each month includes a suggested picture from the *Gospel Art Book* that can be displayed in your home or classroom. You can find the *Gospel Art Book* on LDS.org or in the Gospel Library App. If desired, you can display and refer to this picture throughout the month. Changing it monthly will help keep these lessons fresh in the children's minds.

Weekly Sections

SCRIPTURE

The weekly scripture reference is meant to help you find scriptures for a child to give as part of a talk in your home or in Primary. You may also want to encourage older children to share an article of faith in addition to the scripture for the week.

TALK

Each week includes a sample talk that would be appropriate for a child to give in your home or in Primary. The stories in these talks can also be used during a lesson or in family home evening or another setting. While the stories and language are intended to be simple, the concepts and doctrine they illustrate are profound. To foster understanding, you may want to have the child giving the talk illustrate a few of the main ideas visually or share how this story relates to his or her own life. At the end of the talk, have the child bear a brief testimony.

LESSON

The lessons included with each week are to help leaders, teachers, and parents prepare for a class lesson or a family home evening. The basic structure of the lessons is to begin with a discussion, followed by an activity, and an application and review. You may wish to use only part of the lesson or modify it to fit the needs of your children.

The Spirit will help you know how best to teach the principles you want to convey.

The lessons have been designed to involve minimal preparation and planning. While they may include some movement or active participation by children, they are also meant to be reverent enough to be done in a church building on Sunday. At times you may need to remind the children that they are in a house of the Lord and that their voices, behavior, and tone should always reflect that. Of course, it's also important to enjoy learning together. Use your best judgment about whether these activities will work for your children.

With a little adaptation, these lessons and activities can be used by a large or small class or family. For example, instead of picking one or two children to volunteer, you may want to let every child in your group have a turn. You will need the Spirit's guidance to help you adapt your planning to fit the children you serve. Remember that each child is a son or daughter of God, and each one wants to be included. If you have children with different abilities or special circumstances, do your best to be sensitive to them, even if it means changing your original plans.

Please note that this book is not meant to supersede or take precedence in any way over the Church's curriculum. It simply contains some additional ideas for busy teachers and parents. Whether you use it in your home, in Primary, or in another setting, I hope it will be a helpful resource to you so that you can spend your limited time focusing on the children you love and the eternal principles they need to learn.

Chapter 1: January

HEAVENLY FATHER PLANNED FOR ME TO RETURN TO HIM

MULTIMEDIA RESOURCES

- Families Can Be Together Forever (Mormon Channel, https://www.youtube.com/watch?v=0J-_f4oRuWI)
- Who Is Jesus?: A Bible Story for Children (Mormon Channel, https://www.youtube.com/watch?v=qH5HIPl0hRo)

SONG LIST

- Come, Follow Me (*Hymns*, no. 116)
- A Child's Prayer (12)
- Jesus Once Was Little Child (55)
- I'm Trying to Be like Jesus (78)

GOSPEL ART BOOK

1 "Jesus Christ"

Week 1:
I Want to Become like
My Heavenly Father

SCRIPTURE

Moses 1:39

TALK

Ella loves going horseback riding with her dad. They get to explore new trails together, and he shows her all the places where he loved to ride when he was young. It takes a lot of hard work to care for their horses, but Ella and her dad work together to make sure the horses have food and water and a clean place to live. Ella loves spending time with her dad. She wants to be just like him when she grows up.

Ella knows she has another father, her Heavenly Father. Heavenly Father is the father of Ella's spirit. Heavenly Father loves Ella and He loves each one of us because we are His children. He cares about us and the things we are doing. We can talk to our Heavenly Father when we pray. We can tell Him all the things we are thinking about, and we can ask for His help each day. When we make good choices, we can become more like our Heavenly Father.

Our Heavenly Father created this earth for us. He wanted us to have a beautiful place to live and learn new things. He sent us to our families. Heavenly Father gave each of us a family because being part of a family helps us to grow. Through His plan, He made it possible for us to live with our families forever. Heavenly Father wants us to make good choices so we can return and live with Him and with our families forever. Then we can truly be like Him.

LESSON

Discussion: Tell the children that you will be talking about an important journey. It is the journey we are all taking back to our Heavenly Father. Explain that we are in the middle of this journey right now. We do not remember the beginning, and we still have a long way to go, but we know where we are heading, and we know how to get there. Help the children understand that as we make good choices on our journey back to our Heavenly Father, we are becoming more and more like Him.

Activity: Show the children a suitcase or a bag. Ask a few children to come to the front of the room and share something they would take with them if they were going on a long trip. Then help each child name something we should bring with us as we journey through life back to our Heavenly Father. Some examples might be our testimonies, the scriptures, and our relationships with our families. Have each child who shares something help you pack a small object into your suitcase or bag.

Application and Review: Share with the children how much Heavenly Father wants them to make good choices so that they can return to Him and become like Him. Testify of the power and hope that comes from knowing and following His plan. Encourage them to stay on the path back to their Heavenly Father and to help each other on their journey.

Week 2:
Jesus Can Help Me Return
to Heavenly Father

SCRIPTURE

John 11:25

TALK

Here on earth, nothing stays perfect forever. The flowers that come in springtime are gone by the fall. The snowmen we make in the winter have to melt. And no matter how many times we clean our rooms, they always get messy again.

People are the same way. None of us can be perfect. We can try our best, but there is no way we can become perfect on our own. Heavenly Father knows that we can't do it alone. That's why He sent His Son to help us. Jesus came to earth to set an example for us. He also died for us. This was called the Atonement. The Atonement makes it possible for us to become perfect. When we make a mistake, we can repent, and the Atonement will make it better.

Jesus and Heavenly Father love us. They want us to become perfect so we can live with Them again someday.

LESSON

Discussion: Explain to the children that Heavenly Father sent us to earth so that we could learn. We each chose to come here as the first step of Heavenly Father's plan. Now we are doing all we can to learn and become better so that we can return to live with Heavenly Father. But each of us needs help as we journey back to Him. Ask the children who they think can help them on this journey. Explain that we have many helpers, but our most important helper is Jesus Christ. He can lead the way back to Heavenly Father.

Activity: Ask for a volunteer to come to the front of the room. Point to another part of the room and have the child walk there without any assistance. Then, blindfold the child and ask them to return to the front of the room, without peeking. Be sure to stay near the child so they don't trip or get hurt, but do not allow the child to hold onto you.

Take the blindfold off, and have the first child return to their seat. Repeat the activity with another volunteer, but this time, after you put the blindfold on, have a third volunteer come and lead the blindfolded child back to the front of the room.

Application and Review: Tell the children that we cannot see the way back to Heavenly Father on our own. We need Jesus to guide us so that we don't get lost or hurt. Help the children understand that Jesus wants to help each one of us return to live with Heavenly Father. He will always guide us if we ask Him for His help.

Week 3:
I Want to Follow Jesus

SCRIPTURE

John 14:6

TALK

Moses had a hard job to do. He needed to lead his people, the Israelites, all the way from Egypt to the promised land. God knew that Moses would need help, so He gave Moses and the Israelites some special signs that would show them the right way to go. During the day, God gave the Israelites a pillar of clouds that led them in the right direction. And at night a pillar of fire lighted their way.

Today we don't have pillars of fire or clouds to show us which way to go. But we do have a special kind of light that comes from Jesus. It is called the light of Christ. Whenever we need to make a choice, the light of Christ helps us to remember what Jesus did. We can always use the light of Christ to follow Jesus and do what He would do. That is the way we stay safe on our journey back to Heavenly Father.

LESSON

Discussion: Show the children picture 37 from the *Gospel Art Book*, "Calling of the Fishermen." In your own words, share the story of Jesus calling His Apostles to come and follow Him. Ask the children what it means to follow someone.

Activity: To help the children understand that following someone means doing something that they do, sing the song, "Do As I'm Doing" (276). Invite the children to take turns choosing an action and coming to the front of the room to demonstrate that action for the rest of the children.

Application and Review: Have the children sit down again and ask them what kinds of things Jesus did. For each thing they mention, ask them how we can follow Jesus's example and do that thing also. Invite the children to think of one thing they could do this week to follow Jesus.

Week 4:
Following Jesus Leads Me
to Heavenly Father

SCRIPTURE

2 Nephi 2:25

TALK

Lots of things make Ryan happy. He's happy when he gets to go to the park. He's happy when he eats fruit snacks. And he's always happy to go swimming or play in the water. It's good to be happy. There's a verse in the scriptures that tells us that Heavenly Father and Jesus created us so that we could have joy.

Things like parks and fruit snacks can make us happy for a little while, but Jesus knows what will make us happy forever. He knows that we will only be happy forever if we can return to live with our Heavenly Father someday. Heavenly Father lives in a beautiful place called heaven. It is a place where we can feel peace and love. But the only way to get to heaven is to follow Jesus Christ. If we try our best, Jesus leads us step by step. He shows us what to do and how to act. He will lead each of us back to heaven, where we can be happy forever.

LESSON

Discussion: Explain to the children that many people in life are not sure about where they want to go. They may try following several different paths, or they might just wander through life, hoping that in the end, they will be happy. But Heavenly Father wants us to return to Him, and we can't do that by wandering around and hoping to find the right way.

Activity: Invite a few children to come to the front of the room and act out the story of Lehi's family when they found the Liahona and used it to travel through the wilderness and across the ocean to the promised land.

Application and Review: Point out to the children that the Liahona only worked correctly when Lehi and his family were righteous. Remind the children that Lehi had a dream about returning to Heavenly Father. In his dream, only the people who held on tight to the iron rod could find the right way. Explain that Jesus is like our Liahona or our iron rod. When we follow Him, we can know that we will not get lost and that we will travel back to Heavenly Father.

Chapter 2: February

WE CAN ALL FOLLOW HEAVENLY FATHER'S PLAN

MULTIMEDIA RESOURCES

- Our Eternal Life—What Do Mormons Believe? (Mormon Channel, https://www.youtube.com/watch?v=9MiF_HKoFr4&t=40s)
- God's Greatest Creation (Mormon Channel, https://www.youtube.com/watch?v=dMZ-ETxj0hE)

SONG LIST

- Baptism (100)
- I Will Follow God's Plan (164)
- He Sent His Son (34)
- I Am a Child of God (2)

GOSPEL ART BOOK

3 "The Earth"

Week 1:
I Know Heavenly Father
Has a Plan for Me

SCRIPTURE

1 Nephi 3:7

TALK

After Jesus died, many of His Apostles weren't sure what to do. Peter and some of the other Apostles decided to go fishing like they had done before they started following Jesus. Then Jesus appeared to them and told them that they needed to stick to His plan. Jesus said that Peter's mission was not to fish but to lead the church and share the gospel with the people around him.

Jesus has a plan and a mission for you too. Before you were born, Jesus presented the plan of salvation. This plan allows us to return to Heavenly Father after we die. We chose to follow the plan of salvation and come to earth. Now that we are here, each of us has a special mission to perform as we follow the plan of salvation. We can find out what our mission is by reading the scriptures, praying, and listening to the still, small voice.

LESSON

Discussion: Ask the children if they know where we lived before we were born. Explain that each of us lived with Heavenly Father and learned many things there, but we needed to keep learning. The scriptures tell us that we chose to follow Heavenly Father's plan and that He gave us special callings and tasks to do while we were on earth.

Activity: Ask a member of the bishopric or the missionaries in your ward to briefly explain the plan of salvation to the children, including what happened before we were born and what will happen after we die.

Application and Review: Help the children understand that Heavenly Father's plan is for all of us, including each one of them. They have already chosen to follow this plan, and they are on a good path back to Heavenly Father. Share your own testimony of how knowing that Heavenly Father has a plan has helped you in your own life or in your family.

Week 2:
Heavenly Father and Jesus Created Our World

SCRIPTURE

D&C 76:24

TALK

Have you ever seen a beaver dam? It takes beavers a lot of work to make a dam. They have to use their teeth to chop down trees and branches. Then they drag the wood back and put it in place with mud. It takes a lot of work, but once the beavers finish, they have something beautiful and useful.

Heavenly Father wanted to make a beautiful and useful home for His children. Long before we were born, He commanded Jesus to create this world. Jesus worked hard. He knew we would need lots of things here on earth. We would need the sun, the moon, water, land, plants, animals, and many other things. He created all of these for us so we would have a beautiful place to call home. When we see the beautiful things around us, we should remember who made them and give thanks to Heavenly Father and Jesus for creating the earth.

LESSON

Discussion: Explain that Jesus and Heavenly Father created the earth for us to live on and grow here. Share a few of your favorite things They created in nature.

Activity: Ask the children to think of some things that Heavenly Father and Jesus created. Invite one child at a time to come up and draw something Heavenly Father and Jesus created on the board while the other children try to guess what it is. Once the children have guessed, have the child who drew share why they are grateful for this creation.

Application and Review: Tell the children that one way we can show Heavenly Father and Jesus that we are grateful for this beautiful world that They have made us is by taking good care of it. We can also remember to thank Them for the earth when we pray.

Week 3:
Heavenly Father Gave
Me a Body like His

SCRIPTURE

Genesis 1:27

TALK

Leena likes to dance. She has taken lessons since she was little. When she dances, Leena feels excited and happy. She loves to move her body to the music and create something that other people can watch. It takes a lot of energy to dance. Leena is grateful that she has a body so she can dance, run, jump, ride her bike, and do all of the other things she likes to do.

Each of us has a body. Our bodies were created by Heavenly Father and Jesus. All of our bodies are a little bit different. Some people have dark hair and others have light hair. Some people are tall and others are short. But each of us has a body that looks like our Heavenly Father and like Jesus. They created us to look like Them because we are all children of God. When we take good care of our bodies, we show Heavenly Father how much we love Him and how grateful we are for the bodies He gave us.

LESSON

Discussion: Remind the children that last week you talked about how Heavenly Father and Jesus created the earth. Ask them to think about what Heavenly Father and Jesus's greatest creation might be. Have them share a few ideas.

Activity: Tell the children that you're going to watch a video to find out what the greatest creation is. Show the children "God's Greatest Creation" on the Mormon Channel on YouTube. Because some of the words and concepts in this video will be hard for younger children to understand, have them listen for specific parts of the body that Jesus and Heavenly Father created.

Application and Review: Ask the children what it means that our bodies are temples. Share some ideas of how we can take care of our bodies and respect them as temples. Bear your testimony that our bodies look like the bodies that Jesus and Heavenly Father have and that They created us in Their image.

Week 4:
I Can Choose for Myself

SCRIPTURE

2 Nephi 10:23

TALK

Jonah had a choice to make. The Lord asked Jonah to visit the people in Nineveh and tell them that they needed to repent. But Jonah didn't want to do that. Instead Jonah chose to get into a boat and go to a different city. On the way, a storm started. The other people on the ship threw Jonah overboard, and he was swallowed up by a big fish. When the fish put Jonah back on land, Jonah had to make a choice again. This time Jonah chose the right. He went to Nineveh.

Every day we get to make choices, just like Jonah. We can choose to follow the Lord and do what He wants, or we can choose to do whatever we want to do instead. Even if we choose to do something bad, Heavenly Father will never keep us from making choices. He has given us all the gift to choose. This gift is called agency. Agency lets us learn and grow. Without agency, we would never be able to make all the good choices that will someday lead us back to our Heavenly Father.

LESSON

Discussion: Explain to the children that part of Heavenly Father's plan for us involved us coming here to earth where we would experience lots of opposites. Ask the children to name some opposites like light and dark, cold and hot, and so forth. Tell them that one of the most important opposites is the opposite of good and bad. Each time we make a choice, we are free to choose between what is right and good and what is bad or evil. This ability to choose is called agency.

Activity: Hand out paper and crayons to each child. Have older children copy the words "I can choose for myself" at the top of the page. For younger children, help them write the words. Then have the children fold their papers in half and draw a line down the middle. On one side of the paper, have them draw things that represent good choices and on the other side, have them draw things that represent wrong choices.

Application and Review: As the children draw, share with them some examples of choices they could make between bad and good. For example, they could choose good media that helps them feel the Spirit. When they are done drawing, share your testimony that agency is a great gift from our Heavenly Father and that when we use it to make good choices, we can return to live with Him.

Chapter 3:
March

JESUS HELPS US RETURN
TO HEAVENLY FATHER

MULTIMEDIA RESOURCES

- Jesus Is Resurrected (Mormon Channel, https://www.youtube .com/watch?v=MlKetn7ZiNU)
- Where Justice, Love, and Mercy Meet (Mormon Channel, https://www.youtube.com/watch?v=Znzx2HXY8fo&t=42s)
- Tell Me the Stories of Jesus (LDS General Conference, https:// www.youtube.com/watch?v=QRHltbRz7mI)

SONG LIST

- I'm Trying to Be like Jesus (78)
- Did You Think to Pray? (*Hymns*, no. 140)
- Tell Me the Stories of Jesus (57)
- To Think about Jesus (71)

GOSPEL ART BOOK

39 "The Sermon on the Mount"

Week 1:
I Can Learn about Jesus

SCRIPTURE

D&C 19:23

TALK

King Josiah was a young king. He started to rule when he was only eight years old. He wanted to make sure his people were doing what Jesus wanted them to do. So he decided to study the scriptures. As he did, he discovered that some of the things his people had been doing for a long time were not right. King Josiah knew it would not be easy to change. But now that he knew about Jesus for himself, he could not keep doing what was wrong. With King Josiah's help, the people changed and followed Jesus.

Just like King Josiah, you can find out about Jesus for yourself. One way to do this is by studying the scriptures. You should also pray and keep the commandments. When you do these things, you will find out for yourself what Jesus wants you to do. It doesn't matter if you are old or young. Jesus loves you. He wants you to learn about Him so that someday you can become as happy as He is.

LESSON

Discussion: Ask the children what they know about Jesus. Invite one or two children to share their favorite story from His life or His teachings. Share your own favorite story and what it teaches you about Him.

Activity: To help the children learn more about Jesus, display several pictures from the *Gospel Art Book* around (see the table below). Write the titles for the pictures on pieces of paper and hide them around the room. Invite one volunteer at a time to look for a caption. When the volunteer finds a caption, have the children help you identify which picture it belongs with. As you find each caption, share the stories these pictures depict and what they teach us about Jesus.

GOSPEL ART BOOK NUMBER	TITLE
30	The Birth of Jesus
35	John the Baptist Baptizing Jesus
40	Jesus Calms the Storm
42	Christ Healing the Sick at Bethesda
43	Jesus Walking on the Water
50	Triumphal Entry

Application and Review: Encourage the children to continue learning about Jesus by reading the scriptures, talking with their parents, and participating in class. Help the children understand that learning about Jesus helps us become more like Him.

Week 2:
Jesus Atoned for Me

SCRIPTURE
Psalm 24:3–4

TALK

Zane loves to play in the sandbox. But sometimes instead of building sand castles or digging holes, all Zane wants to do is throw the sand around. This makes a big mess. When Zane throws sand, it gets stuck in his hair, on his clothes, and even in between his toes.

Then Zane's mommy always makes him take a bath to get all the sand off of him so he can be clean again.

When our bodies get dirty, we need to take baths. Sometimes our spirits can get dirty too. This happens when we do something wrong or make a mistake. Jesus knows how to make our spirits clean again. He wants us to tell Him when we do wrong so that He can help us to be clean. This is called confessing our sins. Then Jesus wants us to forsake our sins. That means that we promise never to make that mistake again. When we confess and forsake our sins, we show Jesus that we want to be clean and happy just like He is.

LESSON

Discussion: Ask the children if they've ever seen what happens when a red shirt or sock gets into a load of white laundry. Have an older child read Isaiah 1:18. Then explain what this verse means. Share with the children that Jesus Christ made it possible for us to have our sins forgiven through His atoning sacrifice. This means that we don't need to live with our red marks or sins. We can experience that clean white feeling again through repentance.

Activity: Reinforce the concept of becoming clean through the Atonement by drawing a person or a stick figure on the board. Then list some mistakes this person has made. For example, getting angry at a friend or forgetting to say prayers. Each time you list a mistake, draw a frowny face around the person. Have the children help you think of some more mistakes to add to the board. Then explain that this person is ready to repent and feel happy again. Have the children sing or listen to "I Stand All Amazed" (*Hymns,* 193) while you use an eraser to take away all the frowny faces and draw a smile on the person's face.

Application and Review: Bear your testimony of the happiness and joy we can feel when we repent and use the enabling power of Jesus Christ's Atonement to become better people.

Week 3:
I Can Be Resurrected, like Jesus

SCRIPTURE

Mosiah 16:8

TALK

Jesus is like the sun. He gives us light so we can see. He helps us feel warm and happy inside. And there is another way that Jesus is like the sun. Every night, we watch the sun go down. And every morning the sun comes back up again. When Jesus died, it was like the sun going down. Many people who knew and loved Jesus were sad. They did not understand that He would be resurrected. It was like they thought the sun would never rise again.

Then three days later, Jesus did rise again. His body and spirit were joined together. His friends were happy. They knew Jesus had overcome death. Because Jesus was resurrected, each of us will be resurrected too. Our bodies and spirits will be joined together forever in a new, perfect resurrected body. Each time we see the sun rising, we can remember how Jesus was resurrected and how someday we will be resurrected too.

LESSON

Discussion: Read 1 Corinthians 15:20, 22. Ask the children what they think Paul meant when he said that we would all be "made alive in Christ." Explain that after we die all of us will be resurrected. This is an important part of Heavenly Father's plan, and it is only possible because Jesus overcame death. He was the first person to be resurrected. That is why Paul called Him "the firstfruits of them that slept."

Activity: Help the children memorize 1 Corinthians 15:22 by repeating it several times. You may wish to divide the room in half and have half of the children say the first part of the verse and half of the children say the second part. Then switch the two sides. Invite one or two children to come to the front of the room and repeat the scripture and reference.

Application and Review: Share with the children that knowing we will be resurrected someday can change how we live our lives. We know that death is not the end. Our spirits continue living after we die, and someday our spirits and bodies will be reunited and we will be given perfect resurrected bodies that we can keep forever.

Week 4:
I Want to Be Reverent
Because I Love My Savior

SCRIPTURE

Leviticus 19:30

TALK

Jesus was in a boat with His Apostles. He decided to rest. But while He was sleeping, a storm came up. The Apostles were afraid the boat was going to sink. They woke Jesus up and asked Him to help. Jesus told them not to be afraid. He calmed the storm, commanding the waves and winds to be still.

The Apostles were amazed at how quickly the storm stopped. They knew Jesus had great power, but they couldn't believe even the winds and waves would obey Him. The waves and winds obeyed Jesus because He created them. He is their Master just as

27

He is our Master. The difference between us and things in nature is that we get to choose if we will obey Jesus or not. He will never force us to obey Him. But we can show Him how much we love and respect Him by being still and calm when we visit His house. Being reverent at church helps us to learn more while we are there and feel closer to Jesus.

LESSON

Discussion: Ask the children how they show their parents that they love them. Then ask how they show Jesus that they love Him. Since Jesus is not here with us, we cannot give Him hugs or color Him pictures, but we can still show Him that we love Him, and one of the ways we do that is by being reverent when we come to church. Reverence helps us to feel and learn from the Spirit.

Activity: Play a game of reverence tag. This is similar to freeze tag. Play some church music on the piano or another instrument. While the music is playing, have the children talk and move around the room. But then have the music stop abruptly. As soon as the music stops, have the children stop talking, quickly return to their seats, fold their arms, and sit quietly until the music starts again. Practice this a few times until the children can do it without giggling. Be sure to give praise to children who are especially reverent.

Application and Review: Emphasize that being reverent does not mean being completely silent, and it does not mean quietly daydreaming. When we are reverent, we are still paying attention so we can learn. Since church is one of the places we learn to be reverent, let the children know that you will continue to help them practice reverence so that they can feel the Spirit and show respect for Jesus and Heavenly Father when they go to church.

Chapter 4: April

HEAVENLY FATHER GAVE ME A FAMILY

MULTIMEDIA RESOURCES

- Musical Presentation: The Family Is of God (LDS General Conference, https://www.youtube.com/watch?v=GIyHi_bMTxE)
- Why Are Families Important? (Mormon.org, https://www.youtube.com/watch?v=ZpoA6vGbigA)

SONG LIST

- Faith (96)
- I Feel My Savior's Love (74)
- Jesus Has Risen (70)
- Quickly I'll Obey (197)

GOSPEL ART BOOK

Pick one:

- 33 "Jesus Praying with His Mother
- 113 "Payment of Tithing"
- A picture of your own family or another family in your ward.

Week 1:
Heavenly Father's Plan
Is All about Families

SCRIPTURE

The Family—A Proclamation to the World, paragraph 7, sentences 1 & 2

TALK

Before we were born, we lived in heaven with God. There Jesus presented a plan to all of us. Jesus said that we would come to earth and learn to make good choices so that someday we could return to heaven and live there with God again after we died. We all wanted to follow Jesus's plan. The most important part of this plan was that while we were on the earth, we would be part of a family. We need our families to teach us how to choose the right and to keep us safe.

Think about all the things your family helps you with. You need your family, and your family needs you. You could help your family to follow Jesus's plan by learning about your ancestors and preparing to go to the temple someday. You can also help your family choose the right by being a good example.

LESSON

Discussion: Review the plan of salvation with the children. Explain that this plan is not just for individuals. It is for whole families to come together and be sealed forever. Tell the children that this month you will be talking about the different roles we play as members of a family. Discuss how right now, their role is to be children and love and obey their parents. But someday, they will be parents and husbands or wives who teach their own children what is right. Encourage them to prepare now so they can go to the temple someday and be sealed to their own families.

Activity: Give each child a piece of paper and a crayon. Have them draw a picture of a temple with their family outside it. Encourage them to add more family members like their grandparents, aunts and uncles, and cousins.

Application and Review: Show the children a picture of your family. Explain how your ancestors prepared the way for you to follow Heavenly Father's plan and how you're trying to continue following the plan with your own family.

Week 2:
Parents Love, Serve,
Protect, and Teach

SCRIPTURE

Mosiah 4:14–15

TALK

Mother birds spend a long time sitting on their eggs to keep them warm. Then, when it's time for them to hatch, the mother watches patiently as her babies figure out how to crack open their eggs. While they're still little, their mother gathers food for them and feeds them in the nest. And once they're old enough, she teaches them how to fly.

People parents take care of their babies too. Heavenly Father has said that parents are supposed to take good care of their children, both physically and spiritually. This means that your parents should take care of your body, by making sure you have enough food to eat and clothes to wear. And they should take care of your spirit, by teaching you about Jesus and how to feel the Holy Ghost so you know how to choose the right.

I am grateful for good parents, who are teaching me to follow Heavenly Father's plan.

LESSON

Discussion: Remind the class that this month you are learning about the different roles we play as members of a family to help our families return to Heavenly Father. Tell the children that today you will learn what parents need to do to help their families follow Heavenly Father's plan.

Activity: The Family Proclamation outlines the duties of parents, as listed below.

1. Husbands and wives should love and care for each other and their children.
2. Parents should rear children in love and righteousness.
3. Parents should provide for their children's physical and spiritual needs.
4. Parents should teach children to love and serve one another.
5. Parents should teach children to keep the commandments.
6. Parents should teach children to obey the law.

Assign each child one of these duties, and have them come to the front of the room and act out an example of this for the rest of the class.

Application and Review: Share the words to the Primary song "Love Is Spoken Here." If time permits, you could have the children sing this song. Share with the children how grateful you are for good parents and how you are trying to be a good parent. (Note: Even if you do not have children of your own, you can share how you are helping the parents around you with their roles by teaching the children in class.)

Week 3:
I Can Obey My Parents

SCRIPTURE

Exodus 20:12

TALK

At Millie and Hattie's house there are a lot of rules. There are rules about how long you can watch TV or play on the iPad. There are rules about what you can and can't eat for dinner. And there are rules about when your chores need to be done. Sometimes it seems to Millie and Hattie like there are so many rules they can't even keep track of them all. The girls do their best to follow the rules, but sometimes they make mistakes.

It's okay to make mistakes sometimes, but we should all try our best to follow the rules our parents give us. We might not always like the rules, but rules keep us happy and safe. Parents make rules because they want their kids to learn. Heavenly Father does the same thing. He gives us rules called commandments so that we can learn how to return to Him. One of Heavenly Father's commandments is to obey your parents. So when you follow your parents' rules, you are obeying them and Heavenly Father at the same time!

LESSON

Discussion: Remind the children that this month you are learning about the different roles that members of a family play. Last week you talked about what parents can do to help their families follow Heavenly Father's plan, and this week, you will discuss what children can do. One of the most important things children do is learn to obey their parents.

33

Activity: To practice obedience, play the game "Simon Says," but substitute "Mom" or "Dad" in place of "Simon." Invite older children to take turns giving the instructions.

Application and Review: Emphasize that it is important to follow our parents' instructions about physical and spiritual rules. When we obey our parents, we will be happier, and our families will grow stronger.

Week 4:
I Love and Serve My Family

SCRIPTURE

John 13:34

TALK

Some people have big families, and some have small families. Ruth's family was very small. After Ruth's husband died, the only people in Ruth's family were Ruth and her mother-in-law, Naomi. One day, Naomi decided to go back to her homeland. She told Ruth she was leaving. Ruth wanted to go with Naomi. She loved Naomi because Naomi was part of her family. So Ruth and Naomi traveled to Naomi's home and lived there together.

We need to love our family members too. Whether we have big families or little families, we need to show the people in our families that we love them. We can show our love by doing nice things and by being obedient, respectful, and kind. We also need to tell the people in our families that we love them.

LESSON

Discussion: Remind the children that you have been learning about the different roles members of the family play to help their families follow Heavenly Father's plan. Parents love, serve, protect, and teach. Children honor and obey their parents. And today you will talk about how children can also love and serve the other members of their families.

Ask the children how they show love to the people in their families. Encourage them to think of service as a way to show love. List their ideas on the board.

Activity: Help the children serve in their families this week by creating a service bingo board. Fold a paper into sixteen sections by folding it in half four times. (For younger children, you may want to only use eight sections.) In each section, have the children write or draw something they can do to serve their family members. Use the list on the board to help the children think of more ideas. It is also okay to repeat ideas and use them on multiple days.

Application and Review: Encourage the children to keep their service charts throughout the week and add stickers or color in each section when they give service in that way. Share with the children how giving service to others helps you to love them, especially in your own family.

Chapter 5:
May

MY FAMILY CAN
FOLLOW THE PROPHET

MULTIMEDIA RESOURCES

- We Need Living Prophets (Mormon Channel, https://www.youtube.com/watch?v=j8nSv95wXyM)
- Mormon Prophets | Now You Know (Mormon Channel, https://www.youtube.com/watch?v=PmeXMEhFIYA)
- Why Do We Have Prophets? (Mormon.org, https://www.youtube.com/watch?v=8SBxUcV1L7A)

SONG LIST

- Keep the Commandments (146)
- Families Can Be Together Forever (188)
- I Am a Child of God (2)
- Latter-day Prophets (134)

GOSPEL ART BOOK

138 "Russell M. Nelson"

Week 1:
Heavenly Father Speaks
to Prophets

SCRIPTURE

Amos 3:7

TALK

Allison likes to play soccer. She knows that when she's playing she needs to listen to her coach and do what she says. Allison's soccer coach has played soccer herself, so she always has good advice. Her coach can also see how the whole game is going. Allison can only see what's happening on her part of the field. Allison has learned that she needs to trust the things that her coach tells her and do her best to follow the coach's instructions.

Each one of us has someone who can be like a coach for us. This person is our prophet. Because they communicate with Heavenly Father, prophets can see things that we can't see on our own. Prophets tell us how to live so that we can be happy. They know how to follow Jesus because they do it themselves. We need to learn to listen to our prophet so that we can hear what he is telling us to do. Listening to the prophet is so important because it's like listening to Heavenly Father.

LESSON

Discussion: Ask the children if they know what a search engine is. Explain that a search engine is something we use to find things online. We can ask questions and find answers, or we can look for more information about topics that interest us. A search engine uses powerful technology to locate data from all over the internet and return it to us instantly on our phones or computers.

Sometimes it finds information that we don't want or need, but most of the time, if we give it the right instructions, it will give us the right information. Explain that prophets are sort of like search engines, except that instead of giving us information from the internet, they give us information from Heavenly Father. Without a prophet, we would have no one with the authority to ask Heavenly Father the important questions we need to know about in our day. And Heavenly Father would not have someone to give answers to so that person could share the information with everyone else. Just like it would be hard to find the right answers on the internet without a search engine, it would be hard for us to find the right answers to our questions in life if we did not have a prophet to bring us the correct information from Heavenly Father.

Activity: Help the children learn to listen to and love the prophet by watching the YouTube video "Special Witnesses of Christ— President Russell M. Nelson" (Mormon Channel, https://www .youtube.com/watch?v=YRwQzKe-5lo).

Application and Review: Ask the children what they have learned from listening to prophets. Share your testimony of the prophet and his important role in our church and in your own life.

Week 2:
My Family Can Learn from the Prophets in the Scriptures

SCRIPTURE

1 Nephi 19:23

TALK

Do you have a scripture hero? Many people think of Nephi, Moroni, or Joseph Smith as scripture heroes. These men were righteous and heroic, but they couldn't have done everything they did without the help of some very important people—their families.

Nephi taught his brothers how to understand the scriptures. Moroni and his father wrote letters to encourage each other. And Joseph Smith relied on his family to help him spread the news about the true gospel.

We can follow the example of these scripture heroes by loving and serving the people in our family. Families are so important to Heavenly Father. He knows that we will only be happy forever if we can be with our families. That's why He told the prophets in the scriptures what to say to us so that we can make good choices that will help us live with our families eternally.

LESSON

Discussion: Ask the children to name some prophets they know from the scriptures. You may want to list these on the board. Discuss why Heavenly Father gave us the scriptures and why He wanted the prophets who lived long ago to record their words for us to read. Explain that even though some of the scripture prophets lived many thousands of years ago, they had families just like we do, and they taught their families to choose the right. Even though

39

the world has changed a lot since they lived, we can still learn from their words today.

Activity: Assign each child a scripture from the table below. Have the child read the scripture and identify the prophet. Then have the class discuss what we can learn about having a happy family from the teachings or example of their scripture prophet. When they are done talking, have each child share what they learned with the class. You may wish to show the corresponding *Gospel Art Book* picture on the board while the children are speaking. Ask the children how what they learned from their scripture prophets can help their families today.

PROPHET	SCRIPTURE REFERENCE	GOSPEL ART BOOK
Noah	Genesis 7:1, 5, 23	8 "Noah and the Ark with Animals"
Samuel	1 Samuel 3:8–10, 19–21	18 "Boy Samuel Called by the Lord"
Elijah	1 Kings 18:36–39	20 "Elijah Contends against the Priests of Baal"
The Brother of Jared	Ether 3:6–13	85 "The Brother of Jared Sees the Finger of the Lord"
Nephi	1 Nephi 17:49–52	70 "Nephi Subdues His Rebellious Brothers"
Moroni	Moroni 10:5–6	86 "Moroni Hides the Plates in the Hill Cumorah"

Application and Review: If time permits, sing one or two verses of "Follow the Prophet" (110). Testify that the words of the prophets in the scriptures can still help us and our families today.

Week 3:
Following the Prophet
Blesses My Family

SCRIPTURE

D&C 1:38

TALK

Owen's dad used to go to work every day, but right now he doesn't. Owen knows his dad wants to go back to work. He is looking for a new job. But for now, Owen's family has made some changes. Instead of going out to eat dinner at a restaurant, they stay home every night and use the extra food they have in their food storage.

Having food storage is one way to follow the prophet. Prophets teach us to be ready for the future by paying our tithing, storing extra food, and saving money. They also teach us to be kind to others, to go to school and learn as much as we can, and to make good choices about the media we watch and listen to.

Owen's family is grateful that they followed the prophet by paying their tithing and saving food and money. When we follow the prophet, we are always blessed.

LESSON

Discussion: Remind the children that this month you are learning about how to follow the prophet. Ask them if they know why we have prophets now instead of having everyone learn and study the gospel on our own or only having the stories of prophets in the scriptures. Explain that we need a prophet because he is the only one with all the keys and authority to lead our church and do Heavenly Father's work here on the earth. We also need a prophet now so he can teach us what Heavenly Father wants us to do in our day. When we do what he says, we are blessed.

Activity: Ask an older sister or couple in your ward to come to your class or home and share how following the prophet has blessed their family. Invite them to bring a photo of their children and grandchildren, since the children may not know them. Ask the children to listen carefully while your guest or guests are speaking and try to identify specific blessings that come from following the prophet.

Application and Review: Invite the children to share the blessings they heard that come from following the prophet. Share a few that you heard as well. Remind the children that following the prophet is part of how we follow Heavenly Father's plan so we can return to live with Him forever with our families. Briefly share your testimony of how following the prophet has blessed you and your family.

Week 4:
I Can Listen to the Prophet at General Conference

SCRIPTURE

D&C 21:5

TALK

King Benjamin was the king of all the Nephites. He wanted to tell his people some important things about the gospel, so he planned a special meeting. All of his people brought their tents to the meeting so they could stay and listen. This meeting was a lot like the general conferences we have today. General conference is a special time. It only happens twice a year. We don't bring tents and camp in temple square, but we do try to prepare for general conference. We try to make sure we aren't doing anything on those days, and we think about questions we might have about the Church or our lives.

We are so blessed to have living prophets to guide us, and we are blessed when we listen to them reverently during conference and then try to do what they say.

LESSON

Discussion: Ask the children to help you think of some things the prophet told us to do at the most recent general conference. You may need to help younger children to think of some ideas.

Activity: As a group, choose one thing the prophet told us to do that you all want to focus on doing better. Invite the children to draw a picture to help them remember what they are going to try to do better. Somewhere on the page, help them write the words, "I Can Follow the Prophet."

Application and Review: Encourage the children to share their commitment to follow the prophet with their parents and other family members this week. Remind them that even though they are young, the prophet's words are for them, and they can listen to and obey the prophet just as they would listen to and obey Jesus if He were here on the earth.

Chapter 6:
June

MY FAMILY IS BLESSED BY THE PRIESTHOOD AND TEMPLE WORK

MULTIMEDIA RESOURCES

- Spiritual Dynamite (Mormon Channel, https://www.youtube.com/watch?v=uSaiX7sCDV0)
- Standing in Holy Places (LDS Youth, https://www.youtube.com/watch?v=Oj9jpAlZX48)

SONG LIST

- Love One Another (136)
- Behold the Great Redeemer Die (*Hymns*, no. 191)
- Did Jesus Really Live Again? (64)
- Love Is Spoken Here (190)

GOSPEL ART BOOK

121 "Temple Baptismal Font"

Week 1:
My Family Is Blessed
by the Priesthood

SCRIPTURE

D&C 84:19–20

TALK

One time Oliver was climbing trees with his cousins, Louisa and Jane. They were having a great time. But then Louisa slipped and fell from a high branch. Her leg was broken, and she looked like she was really hurt. Oliver went to get help. He watched while his dad and older brother gave Louisa a blessing. He blessed Louisa that she would be okay. Then they took her to the hospital.

Oliver knew Louisa would be all right because his dad had said so in his blessing. Oliver's dad holds the priesthood. The priesthood is the same power Jesus used to perform miracles while He was alive. Someday Oliver will be able to hold the priesthood too. Having the priesthood in our church is a great responsibility, but it is also a great blessing because we can use that power to help others. We are so blessed to have God's power here on the earth. Without the priesthood, we would not be able to perform all of the ordinances that we need to do here in order to return to Heavenly Father someday.

LESSON

Discussion: Ask the children if they have ever lost something very important. Tell them that after Jesus and His Apostles died, something very important was lost. It was something we really need, but it could not be found anywhere. It was the priesthood. Explain that the priesthood is the power of God and that we need it to perform sacred ordinances. Ask the children if the priesthood has ever blessed them. If they have a hard time thinking of when this might have happened, remind them that we use priesthood power during the sacrament, during baptisms, during priesthood blessings, and in the temple. Point out that priesthood power doesn't just bless individually; it blesses our whole family.

Activity: Bring a small ball or another soft object that you can toss around the room. Invite one child to come to the front of the room and talk about how the priesthood blesses his or her family. When the child is done, let them toss the ball to another child in the room. Then have that child come to the front and share. Repeat this activity, pointing out the different ways that the priesthood blesses us. Note that younger children might need some prompting to think of specific blessings, but they will probably still want to participate.

Application and Review: Remind the children that for a long time, the priesthood was not on the earth. This meant that many people did not learn the true gospel or receive the blessings of the temple. Tell them that this month we will be talking about those temple blessings and how to help our family members, even those who lived along time ago, before the priesthood was restored. Invite them to continue looking for more ways that the priesthood blesses their families and to share those thoughts with their parents and siblings.

Week 2:
Temple Work Seals
Families Forever

SCRIPTURE

D&C 132:46

TALK

Yesterday was a special day for Gracie because she and her brother Gavin went to the temple. Their mommy was sealed to her new husband and then Gracie and Gavin were sealed to both of them.

When they got to the temple, Gracie and Gavin played in a special room and watched a movie about the temple. Then it was time to get ready. Gracie put on her pretty white dress and helped Gavin put on his white suit. While they were in the temple, they walked slowly and spoke quietly because they knew that the temple is Heavenly Father's house. After they were done, they went outside and took lots of pictures so they could remember this day for a long time.

The temple lets us every family be sealed together forever. That's why temples are so important. They make it possible for our whole family to be together forever.

LESSON

Discussion: Explain that the temple is where we go to perform sacred ordinances for ourselves and for our ancestors. When we are sealed in the temple, our families can be together forever, even after we die. This means that we are also sealed to all the people in our families who lived before us. Heavenly Father wants us to be able to live with the people we love forever. That's why He has given us temples, where we can be sealed.

Activity: To show the children how temple work links our families forever, help them make a long paper chain that you can display in the room. Bring paper strips or ask older children to cut some paper into strips. Then have the children write the names of people in their family on the strips. If you have a large group, you may want to limit each child to one or two paper strips. Then use tape or a stapler to create links in the chain with the paper strips. Connect all the links together and have the children help you hold it up around the room. Point out that we are all part of the same eternal family because we are all children of God.

Application and Review: Have the children return to their seats and imagine that they are one link in that long paper chain. Explain that their family members need them to stay strong in the gospel so that they can all be sealed together forever. Share your own testimony of the importance of temple work and how being sealed blesses families.

Week 3:
Someday I Can Go to the Temple

SCRIPTURE

Isaiah 2:2–3

TALK

When the pioneers reached Salt Lake City, one of the first things they did was start building a temple. It took them forty years to finish. Stone by stone, they worked. They made many sacrifices for the temple.

Someday each of us can go to the temple. But just like it took the pioneers a long time to build the temple in Salt Lake, it takes us a long time to get ready to go inside the temple. You can start preparing now, while you are still young, to go to the temple someday. It may take a lot of hard work and sacrifice to be able to enter the temple, but it is worth it. In the temple, you can feel so close to Heavenly Father. He will help you to prepare yourself to enter the temple because He wants you to come and be with Him there.

LESSON

Discussion: Ask the children to name some things that we have that people a long time ago did not have. They might list things like electricity, cars, cell phones, or computers. Then display or point to a picture of the temple. Explain that a long time ago there were no temples on the earth, or there might have been only one, and only a few people were allowed to go inside it. Now we are blessed with hundreds of temples where we can perform sacred work and feel closer to Heavenly Father.

Activity: Tell the children that today you're going to help them prepare to enter the temple by having a race to get ready for the temple. Copy the numbered list below onto the board. Demonstrate the actions that correspond with each step. Then have them stand and perform the actions slowly while they say the words of each step. You may need to have them spread out so they have enough room to perform the actions. Repeat the steps several times, going a little bit faster each time. Or think of additional steps and actions and add them to your list.

STEPS TO PREPARE FOR THE TEMPLE	ACTION
1. Learn to Pray	Fold arms and bow head
2. Read the Scriptures	Hold hands open, like a book
3. Attend Church	Put fingertips together and slant arms to form the shape of a church building.

4. Listen to the Holy Ghost	Cup ear with one hand
5. Love and Serve Others	Place hands on chest, then move outward toward others.

Application and Review: Remind the children that preparing for the temple is not something we can do one time and be ready to go. We have to keep making good choices for a long time so that we're ready to make covenants in the temple. Help the children understand that even though it may be a few years until they can perform baptisms for the dead, the good choices they are making now will help them to be ready when they are old enough to enter the temple. Testify that even visiting the grounds of the temple now can help them to feel the Spirit that is there. Share your feelings about the temple and how blessed we are to have so many temples available to us in our day and to be able to go inside and worship there.

Week 4:
I Can Do Family History Work

SCRIPTURE

D&C 128:5

TALK

Brinley loves to read stories about people who lived a long time ago. In the books she reads, the people all wear funny, old-fashioned clothes and hats. Instead of driving in cars, they have to walk or ride horses. Reading books helps Brinley learn about things that happened long before she was born.

One day, Brinley's older brother showed her how to see their family tree on his phone. He showed her pictures of their ancestors, and Brinley recognized some of the old-fashioned clothes and hats she had seen in the books she read. Now Brinley is learning all about the people in her own family who lived a long time ago. They may have worn different clothes and ridden horses instead of riding in cars, but they were real people with real families, just like Brinley and her brother.

You have a family too, and that means you can do family history work. In our church, we know that families are forever. This means that even our ancestors who lived long ago are still part of our families. Our ancestors love us and want us to get to know them better. We can show them we love them and remember them by learning more about them. Learning about our ancestors is called family history work.

LESSON

Discussion: Show the children a picture of your family, ideally one that includes multiple generations. Explain that we have all been given family members on earth that we know and love now, but we have other family members who lived before we were born. They know and love us, just like the members of our family who are alive now. Our ancestors prepared the way for us to have the blessings that we enjoy.

Activity: To help the children get to know their ancestors, have them draw a tree with several branches. Help younger children write their own name at the bottom of the tree. For older children, have them draw themselves and their own immediate family members at the base of the tree and then write the names of any ancestors they know in the branches of the tree. Encourage all the children to show their trees to their parents and ask their parents to help them add more of their ancestors' names in the branches of their trees.

Application and Review: Help the children understand that they can begin to do family history work now by learning stories about their ancestors. Tell them that there are many tools they can use online with help from their parents or older family members to find more information about their families. Testify that when we learn about and serve our ancestors through temple and family history work, we are blessed and so are they.

Chapter 7: July

WHEN I AM BAPTIZED AND CONFIRMED, I BECOME A MEMBER OF GOD'S CHURCH

MULTIMEDIA RESOURCES

- The Restoration (LDS Youth, https://www.youtube.com/watch?v=_MzDz7OXKUE)
- Discovering Truth (Mormon Channel, https://www.youtube.com/watch?v=hXiGaV8tY5M)

SONG LIST

- Stand for the Right (159)
- I'll Walk with You (140)
- I Know My Father Lives (5)
- Search, Ponder, and Pray (109)

GOSPEL ART BOOK

35 "John the Baptist Baptizing Jesus"

Week 1:
Our Church Was Restored

SCRIPTURE

Articles of Faith 1:6

TALK

What does it mean to restore something? When we restore furniture or machines, we take something that is old and clean and fix it until it works like new again. This means that something that has been restored is both old and new at the same time. The same is true for our church.

Joseph Smith wanted to know which church was right, so he prayed. Heavenly Father and Jesus visited him and told him that the churches around him were not working anymore. Instead, Joseph would need to restore the true church. He did this by following the revelations and promptings Jesus gave him.

Now we have a church that is both old and new. It is old because it is the same church that was on the earth long ago. But it is also a new church because it works like new. Just like in older times, our church still helps us learn about Jesus, and it teaches us how to return to Him.

LESSON

Discussion: Invite one of the children to share what they remember about Joseph Smith praying in the Sacred Grove. Explain that this was the beginning of what we call the Restoration. This was a time when the true church of Jesus Christ was brought back to the earth. Through the Spirit, Joseph learned all about the organization and important gospel truths that were part of the church Jesus established when He lived a long time ago.

Activity: Prepare a simple puzzle by cutting up a picture of a Restoration event or simply writing "The Church of Jesus Christ Was Restored" on a piece of paper and cutting that paper into smaller pieces. You will probably want at least five pieces. Show the children the puzzle pieces and then ask for a volunteer. Have the volunteer leave the room while the rest of the children help you hide the puzzle pieces. Invite your volunteer to come back into the room and look for the pieces. While they are looking, point out that Joseph Smith had to study and ask the Spirit for help to find all the pieces of Jesus's church that needed to be restored. Each time a child finds a puzzle piece, invite them to bring it to the front of the room and share something about our church organization or doctrine that was restored by Joseph Smith. Then have the child try to put the puzzle together. Depending on how quickly the children find the pieces, and how many puzzle pieces you have, you may have time to repeat the activity with different volunteers.

Application and Review: Remind the children that our church is the same as the one in Jesus's day. Share your thoughts on the restored gospel and how knowing that we have the true doctrines and power of Christ in our church has helped you to strengthen your testimony.

55

Week 2:
I Want to Be Baptized
and Confirmed a
Member of the Church

SCRIPTURE

Moroni 8:11

TALK

Leo's mom didn't used to go to church. His dad had been baptized a long time ago, but he had stopped going to church too. Then one day the missionaries came to visit Leo's parents. The missionaries asked if they could teach Leo's mom. She said yes. In time, the missionaries invited Leo's mom to be baptized. Leo's mom believed that the Church was true. She wanted Leo to know the truth too. She decided to be baptized.

Their whole family began going to church together. Now that Leo is almost eight, he is excited to be baptized and confirmed just like his mom was. When we are baptized, we become members of the Church. We promise to help each other and to look out for one another. We also receive the Holy Ghost. The Holy Ghost helps us to know the truth. Leo is happy that someday soon he will become a member of the Church just like his parents.

LESSON

Discussion: Invite the child in your class who is closest to his or her eighth birthday to come to the front of the room. Tell the children that turning eight is a special birthday because when you are eight you can choose to be baptized and become a member of the Church. If the child has already been baptized, invite him or her to share their thoughts about that event. If the child has not yet been baptized, invite him or her to talk about what they are looking forward to about being a member of the Church.

Activity: Divide the children into three or four groups. Assign each group a song that has to do with baptism from the table below. Have them discuss what this song teaches about baptism. Then invite the three groups to present what they discussed to the whole class. To do this, they can either sing their song or simply read the lyrics aloud and then share what they talked about regarding what we can learn from this song about baptism.

SONG	PAGE NUMBER
Baptism	100
When I Am Baptized	103
When Jesus Christ Was Baptized	102
I Like My Birthdays	104

Application and Review: Summarize what the groups discussed about baptism. Then tell the children about when you were baptized. Encourage the children who have not yet been baptized to prepare for this event, and invite those who have already been baptized to remember that experience and reflect on how that felt.

Week 3:
The Holy Ghost Is a
Comforter and Guide

SCRIPTURE

3 Nephi 19:9

TALK

One time, Hazel went to the fair with her family. She had a lot of fun looking at the animals and riding on the rides. But then something bad happened. Hazel got lost. She was scared. She couldn't see her family anywhere. And she didn't know what to do. Hazel started to cry.

Then she remembered something she should do. She said a prayer and asked Heavenly Father to help her not to be scared. As she finished her prayer, Hazel felt peaceful and calm. She knew that it was the Holy Ghost. The Holy Ghost is called the Comforter. He works with Jesus and Heavenly Father to keep us safe, help us when we need help, and cheer us up when we're sad.

When Hazel's family found her, she told them all about her prayer. Her family was glad that Hazel was safe, and they were also glad she had felt the peace that comes from the Holy Ghost.

LESSON

Discussion: Tell the children that today you will be talking about a member of the Godhead and invite them to guess who it is. When they guess the Holy Ghost, tell them that's correct and then ask them what they know about the Holy Ghost. Explain that the Holy Ghost can be someone who comforts and guides us.

Activity: Bring a blanket and a flashlight or draw pictures of these objects on the board. Invite a volunteer to come to the front of the room and wrap the blanket around them while they share a story from the scriptures or their own lives about a time when the Holy Ghost was a comforter or a guide. Then have them use the flashlight to choose the next volunteer by shining the light on the feet of someone who wants to come up next. Repeat this activity a few times with new volunteers, as time permits.

Application and Review: Invite the children to pray for comfort and guidance from the Holy Ghost. Remind those who have been given the gift of the Holy Ghost that they have access to His help anytime they need it, as long as they are making good choices.

Week 4:
The Holy Ghost Teaches
Me the Truth

SCRIPTURE

Moroni 10:5

TALK

Korihor said that Jesus and Heavenly Father were not real. When Alma found out about this, he was upset. Alma knew that Jesus and Heavenly Father were real because an angel had appeared to him. Alma asked Korihor why he was telling lies. Korihor said he would stop if God gave him some sort of sign. God took away Korihor's voice so that Korihor couldn't lie anymore. Later Korihor admitted that he had been lying. He said that Satan had appeared to him. Satan had told Korihor those lies. Then Korihor repeated them to the people around him.

We can know if something is true or if it's a lie when we listen to the Holy Ghost. The Holy Ghost always tells the truth. He will never lie. In fact, He couldn't lie even if He wanted to. When you know the truth through the Holy Ghost, it will be much harder for Satan to tell you lies like the ones he told to Korihor.

LESSON

Discussion: Ask the children if they remember who you talked about last week. Remind them that it was a member of the Godhead. When they guess the Holy Ghost, explain that last week you talked about how the Holy Ghost can comfort and guide us, and this week you will discuss how the Holy Ghost reveals truth to us through our minds and our hearts.

Activity: To illustrate the importance of listening to the still, small voice of the Holy Ghost, invite a few children at a time to come to the front of the room and play a game of "telephone." Start by whispering a scripture from the chart below into the ear of one volunteer, with the scripture reference for older children. Then have that volunteer whisper what he or she heard to the next volunteer and so on until you reach the end of the line of volunteers. Have the last child tell everyone what he or she heard and then reveal what the message was when you began.

MESSAGE	SCRIPTURE REFERENCE
"By the power of the Holy Ghost ye may know the truth of all things."	Moroni 10:5
"Behold, I will tell you in your mind and in your heart, by the Holy Ghost."	D&C 8:2
"The Holy Ghost shall teach you all things and bring all things to your rememberance, whatsoever I have said unto you."	John 14:26
"For he that diligently seeketh shall find; and the mysteries of God shall be unfolded unto them, by the power of the Holy Ghost."	1 Nephi 10:19

Application and Review: Help the children understand that, as illustrated by this game, it is better to learn the truth directly from the source of truth, rather than from several other people who have passed the message along. Explain that the Holy Ghost is our source of truth. As we live righteously and have faith, He will reveal truth to us so that we can know what is right and what is wrong. Tell the children about a time when the Holy Ghost revealed truth to you. Share what that felt like and what you chose to do as a result.

Chapter 8: August

LEARNING AND HAVING FUN TOGETHER HELPS MY FAMILY

MULTIMEDIA RESOURCES

- The Mormon Practice of Family Home Evening (Mormon Newsroom, https://www.youtube.com/watch?v=4cq0gQ_gVN0&t=1s)
- What Family Means to Me—Music Video—Jaeden Vaifanua (2017 Mutual Album) (LDS Youth, https://www.youtube.com/watch?v=BNhN5IEXl-M)
- Family Prayer Isn't Just for Praying | Mormon.org (Mormon.org, https://www.youtube.com/watch?v=QxUwhq2esXE)

SONG LIST

- When I Am Baptized (103)
- The Holy Ghost (105)
- The Lord Gave Me a Temple (153)
- Seek the Lord Early (108)

GOSPEL ART BOOK

112 "Family Prayer"

Week 1:
We Can Pray as a Family

SCRIPTURE

3 Nephi 18:21

TALK

Austin is Azucena's little brother. He's only two years old. Austin loves to say prayers, and when he does, he prays for everything. He prays for his trucks and teddy bears. He prays for the trees outside and their pet goldfish. He even prays for the carpet and the windows and the broom. Austin's prayers used to make Azucena laugh a lot. Then their mommy explained that Austin was still learning how to pray and that it was important for Azucena to be reverent. Their mommy said that Jesus listens to every prayer, even if the person praying is only two years old.

The important thing is that Azucena's family says prayers together. When they pray together, everyone in her family feels more love and peace. Saying prayers helps Azucena, Austin, and their sisters and parents to remember Jesus and Heavenly Father. This helps them all to be happier.

LESSON

Discussion: Ask the children to share some of their favorite things to do with their families. Point out that while it's important to have fun as a family, it's also important to learn to pray and feel the Spirit together. When we pray as a family, we grow closer and we have help from Heavenly Father to guide us through life.

Activity: Divide the children into two groups, and hand out small note cards or sticky notes to the children, along with crayons or pencils. Instruct half of the children to write or draw things that they are thankful for on their notes. Have the other half write or draw things they can ask for in their prayers. When they are finished, have the children place their notes on two tables or walls in different parts of the room. Then invite all the children to look at the different note cards. Remind the children that they have many things to be thankful for when they pray to Heavenly Father. Name a few things on the note cards. Then discuss all the things they can ask for when they pray. Encourage the children to think about what they are going to pray for the next time it is their turn to say a family prayer.

Application and Review: Explain that there are many blessings that can come to our families when we pray together. Discuss some of the blessings you have noticed in your family as a result of saying prayers. Help children understand that creating gospel habits in their families when they are young can establish a strong gospel foundation, which will guide them on the path back to Heavenly Father and bless them in their lives for years to come.

Week 2:
We Can Have
Family Home Evening

SCRIPTURE

Matthew 18:20

TALK

Every family is different. Some families have two parents, and some have one. Some families have one kid, and others have a lot more than that. Some families live with grandparents, aunts, uncles, or cousins. No matter how many people are in a family, every family will be blessed for having family home evening.

Family home evening is a special time for a family to be together. But just like every family is different, every family home evening is different too. Some families like to have a lesson and an activity for family home evening. Some like to watch a church movie. Others read stories or play games. And other families go to parks, play sports together, or do craft projects.

That's okay. In fact, the prophets have told us that it doesn't really matter what you do for family home evening as long as you take time to be together and try to feel the Spirit.

LESSON

Discussion: Ask the children to share some of their favorite memories of family home evenings they have had in their families. Share a few of your own as well. Explain that family home evening is a special commandment to spend time together, feel the Spirit, and learn and grow closer as a family.

Activity: Have a few volunteers come to the front of the room to act something out. You may want to give them roles, such as a mother, father, and some children. Tell them they will be acting out a family home evening that is not going so well. Perhaps the children could act bored or distracted by other things. The parents could be frustrated or worried. After a minute or two, have your volunteers pause and ask the rest of the children what the different members of the family could do to make this a better family home evening. Then have the children resume, incorporating the advice of the other children. If time permits, you could repeat this activity with new volunteers.

Application and Review: Discuss with the children the importance of having family home evening regularly. This is something our prophets have asked us to do because it helps us to be stronger as families. Invite the children to be good examples to their families and to encourage the other members of their families, including their parents, to have regular family home evenings so their families can be strong too.

Week 3:
We Can Study the
Scriptures as a Family

SCRIPTURE

Mosiah 1:4

TALK

Nephi's family knew how powerful the scriptures are. After they left Jerusalem, Nephi and his brothers went back to get the brass plates. The brass plates contained the scriptures and other important things that Nephi's family needed to help them on their journey to the promised land. Once they made it to the promised land, Nephi and his family kept reading from the brass plates. The brass plates helped Nephi's children to stay good even when the people around them were being wicked.

The scriptures we have today are just as powerful as the brass plates. When you read the scriptures with your family, you can talk about the gospel and learn from each other. The things you read and talk about will help you, your parents, and everyone you love. The power that comes from the scriptures can keep your whole family happy and safe.

LESSON

Discussion: Hold up a copy of the scriptures and ask the children why they think Heavenly Father gave us scriptures. Explain that even though the scriptures were written a long time ago, they contain many lessons we need to learn in our day. Discuss how the language in the scriptures can be difficult to understand. This is one of the reasons Heavenly Father wants us to study the scriptures as a family. When we read together, we can talk about what the scriptures mean so we can understand them better.

Activity: To help the children think of some other blessings that come from reading the scriptures, listen to the song "Scripture Power" (available on LDS.org). Talk about the blessings that come from reading the scriptures individually and in our families. You may want to list these blessings on the board.

Application and Review: Have the children think of ways they could encourage their families to study the scriptures together. For example, they could volunteer to call everyone to scripture study at a certain time of day, or they could get the scriptures out from wherever they keep them in their house so that they are ready to read. Invite them to follow through on their ideas this week and report how it goes the following week.

Week 4:
My Family Can Keep
the Sabbath Day Holy

SCRIPTURE

Moses 3:3

TALK

Working hard is important. Many people think it is the most important thing in the world. For other people, the most important thing is having fun. They are always thinking about new fun things to do. While it is important to work hard and it's also important to have fun, neither of these are the most important thing in the world.

Heavenly Father taught us what is most important. When He and Jesus created the earth, They worked hard for six days. Then on the seventh day, They rested. This was an example to each of us. We are supposed to work hard and play hard every day except on Sundays. Sundays are a time to remember that the most important things are the things that bring us closer to Heavenly Father. On Sundays we can rest from our work and our play. Instead of focusing on ourselves, we can focus on Heavenly Father. That is how we show Him that we love Him more than anything else in the world.

LESSON

Discussion: Remind the children that you have been talking about some important gospel habits for families this month. Ask them if they would like to report on how they have helped their families pray together, hold family home evenings, and study the scriptures. Encourage them to continue helping their families create and maintain these gospel habits. Then explain that today you will discuss one more habit. Ask them to guess what that habit is. When they guess keeping the sabbath day holy, ask them why the sabbath is a special day. Discuss the importance of Sundays as a day of rest and a time to feel the Spirit without the distractions of our normal routines and activities.

Activity: Pass out papers and crayons to the children. Help them write "Sunday Is Special" at the top of the page on one side of the paper. On this side, have them draw something that their family likes to do on Sunday. Then have them turn their papers over and draw something that their family likes to do on other days of the week on the other side of the paper.

Application and Review: Explain that different families keep the Sabbath day holy in different ways, and that is okay. Each family gets to use the Spirit to help them decide which activities are appropriate for Sunday and which would be better to do on a different day. Encourage the children to share their pictures with their families and to continue to work on those gospel habits in their homes. Share your testimony of the importance of the Sabbath in your own family and how it helps you to live a happy life.

Chapter 9: September

MY FAMILY CAN LIVE THE GOSPEL

MULTIMEDIA RESOURCES

- Shower of Heavenly Blessings (Mormon Channel, https://www.youtube.com/watch?v=8-vXpnKMtUE&index=8&list=PLg9gFw6VpxY5ugclN2DLtxZwJm6eyA6GY&t=0s)
- How Can I Follow Jesus Christ? (Mormon.org, https://www.youtube.com/watch?v=r6CA2AtYkFM)

SONG LIST

- When We're Helping (198)
- A Child's Prayer (12)
- I Know That My Redeemer Lives (*Hymns*, no. 136)
- Dare to Do Right (158))

GOSPEL ART BOOK

115 "Service"

Week 1:
I Am Grateful for
All My Blessings

SCRIPTURE

D&C 78:19

TALK

One of Charlee's favorite things is to make crafts. She works hard to create things that are perfect. And when she's done, she's always excited to show them to her friends and her family. Sometimes she gives the things she makes to other people as presents. Charlee feels great when they tell her thank you for the things she makes.

Heavenly Father likes to create things too. Sometimes He creates things we can see and touch, like beautiful clouds, ocean waves, or strong trees. Sometimes the things He creates are not visible. These are things like love and peace. We need to make sure we thank Heavenly Father for all of the things He creates for us. Heavenly Father loves it when we notice the things He creates and when we are grateful for them. When we pray, we can tell Heavenly Father how much we love the things He makes and how thankful we are to have them.

LESSON

Discussion: Ask the children what kinds of things they like to make. Some might like to draw, while others might like to write or bake or make things out of clay. Tell the children that when we make things, we are being creative. Heavenly Father and Jesus are also creative. In fact, They created the whole earth for us and lots of stars and other planets too. When we do creative things, we are following Their example and learning to become more like Them. We can show Heavenly Father and Jesus that we are grateful for Their creations by taking good care of Their creations. We can also show our gratitude by remembering to thank Them for Their creations when we pray.

Activity: Take a walk outside and point out things that Heavenly Father has made. Depending on the size of your group, you may want to walk in two or three smaller groups. You could have all of the groups walk at the same time with different group leaders, or you could take turns having one group walk while the other children stay in the room and sing "My Heavenly Father Loves Me" (228). When you are all back in the room, ask the children to name some of the things they noticed that Heavenly Father created. Then say a prayer together to thank Heavenly Father for all His creations.

Application and Review: Briefly summarize the story of the ten lepers, and encourage the children to be like the one who remembered to return and thank Jesus for what He had done. Tell them that if they will look for things to be thankful for, they will find lots of blessings, and this will help them to be happier and to remember Heavenly Father and Jesus. Share some things that you are grateful for and bear your testimony that being grateful is a way to show respect and love for Jesus and Heavenly Father.

Week 2:
I Serve God by Serving Others

SCRIPTURE

Matthew 25:40

TALK

Collin's mom works as a nurse, helping to take care of old people at their homes. Sometimes she brings Collin with her when she needs to visit one of her patients. Collin used to be a little nervous around his mom's patients. Some of them cannot speak, and some always seem angry or scared.

One time Collin's mom noticed that he was nervous, so she talked to him about it. His mom explained that she loves to take care of her patients because she knows that when we help others, we are really helping Heavenly Father. She said Heavenly Father has blessed us so much that we need to share our blessings and love with those around us.

Now Collin tries to see his mom's patients the same way that she sees them. Instead of noticing how angry they might seem, he thinks of Heavenly Father. He knows Heavenly Father loves all His children, including Collin, Collin's mom, and each of Collin's mom's patients. When we learn to see all the people around us as children of God, we will always be able to serve and love them because we'll know that we're also serving Heavenly Father.

LESSON

Discussion: Remind the children that King Benjamin taught us that when we serve others, we are really serving our Heavenly Father. Ask the children what it means to serve others and what some examples of service might be.

Activity: Show the video "The Old Shoemaker" (Mormon Channel, https://www.youtube.com/watch?v=pifDZ1hu6gY&t=32s), or watch the video before your lesson and then summarize the story for the children in your own words.

Application and Review: Emphasize that service does not have to be a long or elaborate project. It can be something simple we do to help the people around us. Encourage the children to practice serving others this week and pray for opportunities to serve in simple ways each day.

Week 3:
I Want to Be Honest

SCRIPTURE

Job 27:5

TALK

After Joseph Smith saw Heavenly Father and Jesus Christ, he told his family and friends. Some of them believed him, but some of them did not. Many of Joseph's neighbors were angry with him. They thought he wasn't telling the truth. But Joseph Smith knew what he had seen. He could not deny what had really happened, or he would be lying to himself and to God.

We need to be honest like Joseph was. It can be hard to tell the truth, especially when it makes other people angry. But Joseph Smith knew that the most important thing is not what other people think of us. The most important thing is what Heavenly Father thinks of us. Heavenly Father knows when we are honest, even if know one else knows. He will always bless us when we tell the truth.

LESSON

Discussion: Ask the children if they know what the word "integrity" means. When we have integrity, we are honest about who we are and what we believe. We act the same way whether or not someone is watching. We don't try to cheat or lie because we care more about what Heavenly Father thinks than we do about trying to beat or get ahead of other people.

Activity: Explain to the children you are going to play a game that involves lying. Tell them two true things about you and one thing that is a lie. Then have them guess which one is the lie. Once they guess, have another child do the same. After a few people have played, ask them how it felt when they were lying.

Application and Review: Discuss how lying about something little in a game might feel a little uncomfortable or strange, but lying about something bigger in real life feels even worse, especially since telling one lie often means you need to keep lying or tell even more lies to avoid being caught. Encourage the children instead to always be honest and to have integrity even about little things. Tell them about a time when you told a lie, how that made you feel, and what happened as a result.

Week 4:
I Want to Set a Good Example
by Living the Gospel

SCRIPTURE

1 Timothy 4:12

TALK

When Jesus lived on the earth, He wanted to teach His followers to be good examples for all the other people around them. He told the people that they were like a light. He told them that they needed to shine brightly so that the people around them would be able to see the truth. When we have light, we can see which way is the right way.

You can be a light for the people around you by choosing the right. When they see you making a good choice and how happy you are, they will want to make good choices too. Your example will help others to see the truth about the gospel, just as if you were holding up a flashlight or a candle in a dark place. That's why it's so important for us not to be afraid to make good choices, no matter what. You need to choose the right when lots of people are watching and when it seems like no one will notice.

Your example and light will lead others to the truth so that they can be happy, just like you.

LESSON

Discussion: Talk to the children about what it means to be an example. You might point out some times when we use examples to help us know what to do, like in a dance or exercise class when we watch the teacher first and then try to do it ourselves. Explain that we can all be examples for people who want to know how to be happy and choose the right. Point out that sometimes people can set bad examples that we should not follow. That is why we need to make sure that we set a good example for the people who are following us, like the younger children in your class or our friends at school.

Activity: Divide the children into four groups. Then using the table below, assign each group a scripture story. Have them read it or summarize the story in their own words. As they are doing this, write the following questions on the board for the classes to answer. Then have them share their answers with the entire group.

Questions:
- What was your story?
- Who was the example in this story? (Note that in some stories there may be more than one example.)
- Was it an example of doing something good or bad?
- Who followed the example?
- What was the result?

SCRIPTURE STORY	REFERENCE
Daniel in the Lions' Den	Daniel 6
King Noah and Abinadi	Mosiah 11
The Anti-Nephi-Lehies	Alma 24
Jesus Walking on the Water	Matthew 14:22–33

Application and Review: Remind the children that they can always choose whether to follow someone else's example or not. Even if lots of people are doing something bad, that does not make it the right thing to do. They can also choose what kind of an example they will set for the people around them. Explain that when they choose the right and live the gospel, they are setting a good example, even if it seems like no one notices what they are doing. If time permits, share a story about a time when someone set a good example for you to follow and how that helped you to make more good choices to set an example for others.

Chapter 10: October

THE FAMILY PROCLAMATION HELPS MY FAMILY

MULTIMEDIA RESOURCES

- Proclamation Series: Children (Mormon Channel, https://www .youtube.com/watch?v=2aKo6R7U6pg)
- Going to Grandma's (Mormon Channel, https://www.youtube .com/watch?v=11GgH0Kmc2I)
- I Love to See the Temple (LDS General Conference, https:// www.youtube.com/watch?v=EJNN8RuOJyw)

SONG LIST

- When He Comes Again (82)
- The Church of Jesus Christ (77)
- I Love to See the Temple (95)
- When We're Helping (198)

GOSPEL ART BOOK

120 "Young Couple Going to the Temple"

Week 1:
The Family Proclamation
Is from God

SCRIPTURE

Articles of Faith 1:9

TALK

When Lehi's family was traveling through the wilderness, Heavenly Father wanted to make sure they knew which way to go. He gave Lehi a special tool called the Liahona, which pointed the way they should go. It also had writing on it, which taught Lehi what to do and how to lead his family. But the Liahona only worked when Lehi's family obeyed what it said and followed the directions from the Lord.

Today we have a special tool to help our families. This tool is called the family proclamation. The proclamation came from Heavenly Father, just like the Liahona. If we follow its teachings, our families will be blessed. But it will only work for us if we do what it says. We should follow the family proclamation because it teaches us how to be a happy family here on earth and eternally.

LESSON

Discussion: If you remember the announcement of the family proclamation in conference, tell the story of how you felt when that happened. If you do not, ask another member of your ward who does remember to share that story. Explain to the children that the family proclamation is a message from Heavenly Father for our day.

Activity: If possible, ask the other teachers in your Primary to help you with this activity. Assign each teacher a sentence from the family proclamation, as listed below. Have the teachers first explain their sentences to their own classes. Then have the teachers rotate to different classes until all the classes have learned about all the sentences.

1. "Marriage between a man and a woman is ordained of God and . . . the family is central to the Creator's plan for the eternal destiny of His children."
2. "Gender is an essential characteristic of individual premortal, mortal, and eternal identity and purpose."
3. "The divine plan of happiness enables family relationships to be perpetuated beyond the grave."
4. "Parents have a sacred duty to rear their children in love and righteousness, to provide for their physical and spiritual needs, and to teach them to love and serve one another, observe the commandments of God, and be law-abiding citizens wherever they live."
5. "Successful marriages and families are established and maintained on principles of faith, prayer, repentance, forgiveness, respect, love, compassion, work, and wholesome recreational activities."
6. "We warn that the disintegration of the family will bring upon individuals, communities, and nations the calamities foretold by ancient and modern prophets."

Application and Review: Ask the children to share some of the things they learned about families from the family proclamation. Encourage them to continue discussing these things with their parents and other family members. Testify that our prophets and apostles continue to receive revelation in our day and that Heavenly Father has given us the family proclamation to help us become happier individually and as families.

Week 2:
Marriage Is Part of
Heavenly Father's Plan

SCRIPTURE

D&C 131:2

TALK

Rebekah was a righteous young woman. One evening she met a man at a well who asked her for water. Rebekah gave the man water for himself and all his camels. Later Rebekah found out that Abraham had sent the man at the well to find a wife for Abraham's son, Isaac. Abraham and Isaac were righteous men. Rebekah chose to marry Isaac because she knew it was what Heavenly Father wanted her to do.

Many things have changed since Rebekah was alive. But things like marriage have stayed the same. Heavenly Father still wants us to get married. Through His prophets, Heavenly Father has told us how important it is to find someone righteous to marry in the temple. And He has told us that marriage is meant for a man and a woman. Though many things in our world change, we can be sure that the important things about marriage, families, and Heavenly Father's plan will always be the same. That's because Heavenly Father loves each of us, and He knows what will make us happy now and eternally.

LESSON

Discussion: Ask the children why they think Heavenly Father wants us to get married. Explain that being married helps us to learn new things, and it allows us to have children and to raise them in a good environment. Heavenly Father wants us to do our best to find someone good to marry in the temple and then to work hard together to create a righteous family.

Activity: Invite a newly married couple and a couple who has been married for several years to come and talk about why Heavenly Father wants us to get married and what we can do to prepare for an eternal marriage. Encourage the children to listen for reasons why marriage is important to Heavenly Father.

Application and Review: Help the children understand that a happy marriage is a blessing from Heavenly Father, but it also takes work from us. Encourage the children to make good choices now so that when the time comes for them to be married, they can be ready to go to the temple and be sealed forever.

Week 3:
Happy Families Do
What Jesus Taught

SCRIPTURE

2 Nephi 31:12

TALK

Jesus said that the most important commandment is to love God and the people around us. Benjamin knows that some of the people around him are the people in his own family. Benjamin loves his family. He tries to show his love by listening to his parents and doing what they say. Jesus also taught us to share with others, so Benjamin shares his toys with his little sister. And Jesus taught us to look for ways to help other people. Benjamin tries to help his family by making his bed, cleaning his room, and setting the table.

Some people think that Jesus only taught us how to be good people on our own. They don't understand that everything Jesus taught was to show us how to be happy in our families. Jesus wants us to be part of a family. It is only when we are sealed together as families that we can be happy eternally. Benjamin's family is trying to do the things Jesus taught so that they can be happy now and stay together forever.

LESSON

Discussion: Tell the children that when Jesus lived on the earth, He told many stories, called parables. Each parable teaches us something important about how to live righteously. When we learn from these parables and, in our families, do the things that Jesus taught, our families will be happy.

Activity: Assign class members a parable from the chart below. Ask them to summarize the parables, using the corresponding scripture references. Then have the class discuss how the lessons in the parable apply to our families today. Have the children take turns sharing what they learned with the rest of the class. With older children, you may want to create two columns on the board, one column for the parables and the other for the lessons in them that we can apply in our own families. Then have a scribe write their parable and lessons while the others in the class present verbally.

PARABLE	SCRIPTURE REFERENCE
The Wise Man and the Foolish Man	Matthew 7:24–27
The Ten Virgins	Matthew 25:1–13
The Good Samaritan	Luke 10:25–37
The Sower	Matthew 13:18–23

| The Prodigal Son | Luke 15:11–32 |
| The Talents | Matthew 25:14–29 |

Application and Review: Explain that parables often have multiple levels of meaning, and encourage the children to continue to think about these parables and how they apply to our families. If time permits, ask the children to name some other things Jesus taught, and then share how those teachings have helped your family.

Week 4:
My Family Can Work Together

SCRIPTURE

D&C 88:119

TALK

Paul taught that the church is like a body. Each church member has different role to play, just like each part of the body does something different. Our families are the same. Each person in your family has a special role to play and special things only he or she can add to your family. Just like a hand is different from an eye and a nose is different from a heart, each person in a family is different too.

Heavenly Father sent you to your family because He knew you would be able to help your family. He also knew they would be able to help you. When you and your family work together, you can do great things. Working as a family will show you how each person helps in his or her own way, just like each part of your body does something different but equally important.

LESSON

Discussion: Ask the children why our parents make us do chores or work. Explain that work is actually something that Heavenly Father has given to each of us. He wants us to learn how to work hard and accomplish things so that we can take care of ourselves and not have to rely on others. Working also teaches us to be patient and to value the things that come as a result of our hard work.

Activity: Tell the children that you are going to illustrate something about work. Invite a volunteer to come to the front of the room. Spill some small pieces of paper, beans, or rice on the floor. Set a timer and see how quickly the volunteer can pick up all the spilled things and put them back in a bag or jar that you hold. Have the other children watch this process. When the child is done, stop the timer and ask him or her how it felt to do all that work alone. Then repeat the process but this time invite the first child to ask three or four additional children to come up and work together. Time them again and point out how much faster we can do things when we work together than when we try to do them alone. Ask the children who participated if it's easier to do something by yourself or with other people helping you.

Application and Review: Explain that one of the reasons Heavenly Father has given us families is so that we can learn to work together. When we work together, our love for each other grows, we become better at talking to each other, and we have more unity in our families. Share an experience from your own life when you worked with the people in your family to accomplish something. Then tell the children that you are grateful for the opportunity to work in families to support Heavenly Father in accomplishing His work, which is to help each of us return to live with Him forever.

Chapter 11: November

JESUS TAUGHT US HOW TO HAVE STRONG FAMILIES

MULTIMEDIA RESOURCES

- Substance of Faith (Mormon Channel, https://www.youtube.com/watch?v=QbGhD-FcCS8)
- The Shiny Bicycle (Mormon Channel, https://www.youtube.com/watch?v=ItEsXGhcOEs)
- The Power of Prayer (Mormon.org, https://www.youtube.com/watch?v=WRhLK0TCmiQ)

SONG LIST

- Search, Ponder, and Pray (109)
- Tell Me, Dear Lord (176)
- Kindness Begins with Me (145)
- Help Me, Dear Father (99)

GOSPEL ART BOOK

111 "Young Boy Praying"

Week 1:
Faith Means Believing in Things We Cannot See

SCRIPTURE

Alma 32:21

TALK

Lincoln wants to be an astronaut when he grows up. He loves to look at the stars at night. Lincoln knows that the stars are really much bigger than they look like they are when we see them in the sky. Some of them are a lot bigger than our sun. They are bright and hot and far, far away. Even though Lincoln cannot see what the stars really look like, he believes that they are big because he knows that other people have studied them carefully.

Faith is like that. We don't always have to know something because we see it ourselves. We can believe in things because we know other people have studied them and we believe their words. We can also know things through the Holy Ghost, who tells us what is true.

When we have faith, we can believe in Jesus, even though we have not seen Him. We can read the scriptures and believe that they were written by real people who lived a long time ago. And we can know that Heavenly Father has a plan for us and that He loves each one of us and wants us to live the gospel.

LESSON

Discussion: Show the children a photograph. Explain that cameras record things we can actually see with our eyes. Then show them a painting or an illustration and explain that when an artist creates a picture, it might be based on something that artist has seen with their eyes, or it might be based on something the artist sees in their head. As an example, you might show the children the illustration of "Lehi's Dream" from the *Gospel Art Book* (69). This illustration is based on a dream that Lehi and then Nephi had a long time ago. The artist who painted it did not actually have the same dream, but they imagined what the dream must have been like from reading the account in the scriptures. Tell the children that part of having faith is believing in things that you can't see but that your spirit knows are true. When artists can't see something with their eyes, they use their minds to picture what they want to create. And when we can't see something with our eyes, but we believe in it because the Holy Ghost has testified to our spirits that it's true, we are using our faith to believe, even though we can't see.

Activity: Help the children think of some things they can't see but that they have faith in by the Spirit. Hand out papers and crayons, and invite the children to act like artists and draw pictures of things that they have faith in, even though they have not seen them. You might suggest things like Jesus and Heavenly Father in heaven, a story that happened in the scriptures, or what will happen when Jesus returns to the earth.

Application and Review: Explain that learning things with our spirits, through faith, is a lot like learning things at school. It takes time, and we might have questions about what we learn. That is okay. Jesus has invited us to ask Him questions and to keep learning. If we continue to have faith, He will continue to teach us little by little till we know for sure and have a strong testimony.

Week 2:
I Can Talk to Heavenly Father When I Pray

SCRIPTURE

D&C 136:28–29

TALK

Avery's grandparents are serving a mission in Buenos Aires, a city in South America, which is far away from Avery's house. Avery likes to send them pictures and letters in the mail. Her parents read her the emails they send home. And sometimes they all get to talk on the phone or on their computers. It's always fun when Avery gets to see her grandparents or hear their voices. She loves and misses them.

Heavenly Father loves and misses us too. While we are here on earth, it's sort of like we are all serving long missions far away. We have to be away from our Heavenly Father during our earthly missions, that is how we grow and learn to choose for ourselves. But we can still talk to our Heavenly Father when we pray. Heavenly Father always wants to know what we're doing and how He can help us. That's why He has told us we need to pray always.

LESSON

Discussion: Remind the children that last week you discussed about how faith means believing in something that you cannot see with your physical eyes but that you know with your spirit. Another thing we know with our spirits is that Heavenly Father and Jesus listen when we pray. We can even hear or feel responses from Them if we are reverent and patient. It takes faith to pray because you need to believe that Heavenly Father and Jesus are really there and listening. And it takes faith to believe you can receive answers to your prayers as well. Sometimes we pray out loud, and other times we pray in our hearts or in our minds, but every time we pray, Heavenly Father is listening. He wants to hear from us because He loves us.

Activity: If you have a toy microphone, bring it with you. If you don't have one, you can simply use another object and have the children pretend it is a microphone. Pass your microphone around the room, and invite each child to name something they can talk to Heavenly Father about when they pray.

Application and Review: Encourage the children to say prayers often, whenever they want to talk to Heavenly Father. Share an experience you had when you prayed about something and received an answer to your prayer. Then testify that we always receive answers to our prayers, even if those answers don't come when or how we expect.

Week 3:
I Can Change through Repentance

SCRIPTURE
Helaman 5:11

TALK
Addilynn loves to play dress up. She has lots of costumes. She has a fireman costume, a princess costume, a pirate costume, and a superhero cape. But no matter what costume Addilynn is wearing, she is still the same person on the inside. Many people think they

can change who they are on the inside by changing things like their clothes, where they live, or what they do for fun.

We know that the quickest way to change who you are is through the Atonement of Jesus Christ. The Atonement is the sacrifice Jesus made for us when He died. You use the Atonement to repent when you make a mistake, but you can also use it to help you become a better person. That's because the Atonement can change how you think and feel about something. It works on your mind and in your heart. With the Atonement, you can become exactly the person that Heavenly Father wants you to be.

LESSON

Discussion: Explain that one of the most important reasons Heavenly Father sent us to earth was so that we could learn from our mistakes. Heavenly Father knew that we would all make mistakes. That's why in His plan, Jesus acts as our Savior. This means that because Jesus died for us, we can be redeemed or saved from the mistakes we make. This happens as we repent and have faith.

Activity: Divide the children into two groups. Have an older child in the first group summarize the conversion story of Saul (Paul) while another child does the same with the story of Alma the Younger (see Acts 22 and Mosiah 27). Then have the two groups act out their stories for each other. Talk about the two men as a group. Point out how their hearts, minds, and lives changed after they repented.

Application and Review: Encourage the children to think of repenting as an opportunity to grow rather than a time to feel guilty or discouraged. While we should consider our mistakes so we can learn from them, Heavenly Father and Jesus have made it possible for us to press forward and leave our sins and mistakes in the past (see 2 Nephi 31:20). Even when we make mistakes, we should continue to press forward so that we can keep growing and becoming more like Them.

Week 4:
I Can Forgive and Be Forgiven

SCRIPTURE

D&C 64:9–10

TALK

Job had many blessings. He was righteous, and Heavenly Father had blessed him for being good. Then things changed. Job lost his home, his family, and his money. He also got sick. Job's friends told him he should be angry with Heavenly Father, but Job knew being angry wouldn't help anything. It would only make Job feel even worse.

Sometimes when bad things happen, it can make us angry—especially when it's someone else's fault. But Jesus taught us that we should let Him take care of the bad things. He knows what is fair, and He will work it out. So instead of getting angry, our job is always to forgive. We need to forgive other people when they make mistakes so that Heavenly Father will forgive us when we make mistakes.

And you should remember to forgive yourself too. When you make a mistake, you should repent. Then you should stop worrying about the mistake you made and trust Jesus to make things right. Learning how to forgive and be forgiven can be hard at first, but it is the only way to feel real peace.

LESSON

Discussion: Remind the children of the stories of Alma the Younger and Paul that they acted out last week. Ask them to think about how the people around Paul and Alma reacted to these dramatic changes. Some people may not have understood the change. Some people who had been hurt by these men before they repented would have had to forgive them. Explain that forgiving means that instead of focusing on bad things that happened in the past, we focus on how someone feels right now and how they want to be in the future. Sometimes we will need to forgive other people when they make mistakes that hurt us. And sometimes we will need to forgive ourselves when we make mistakes that hurt our spirits.

Activity: Help the children practice forgiveness by talking through some simple scenarios from the list below.

1. Sadie borrowed a toy from Lucas without asking and broke the toy. (Ask the children how the Sadie and Lucas might feel and what they should do. How will forgiveness make Sadie feel? How will forgiveness make Lucas feel?)
2. Nora feels bad about being irreverent during the sacrament. (Ask the children what Nora should do and how forgiveness will make her feel. Point out that sometimes we need to forgive ourselves when we make mistakes and have faith that Heavenly Father has forgiven us too.)
3. Mason got angry at his little brother. He yelled and hit him. Now Mason feels sorry for what he did.
4. Jack worked really hard to draw a picture for his grandpa, but then his sister accidentally spilled juice on the picture.
5. Amelia was supposed to feed her puppy before school, but she forgot, and her mom had to do it instead. This makes her mom frustrated.

Application and Review: Point out that in each scenario, forgiving helps everyone feel happier and not forgiving only makes things worse. Make sure the children understand that it is okay to feel sad or upset when someone hurts them, even if it's just an accident. Sometimes it takes time for us to be able to forgive, and that is okay too, but we should remember that Heavenly Father has promised that if we forgive others, He will forgive us. He wants us to learn how to forgive because He knows that forgiving helps us to focus on the present and the future instead of staying stuck in the past. Share your own feelings about forgiveness and how the Atonement of Jesus Christ makes it possible for us to forgive and trust Heavenly Father.

Chapter 12: December

I WANT TO WORSHIP JESUS

MULTIMEDIA RESOURCES

- Glad Tidings of Great Joy: The Birth of Jesus Christ (Mormon Channel, https://www.youtube.com/watch?v=xCxV9CbC180&t=1s)
- That They Do Always Remember Him (Mormon Channel, https://www.youtube.com/watch?v=oXio1W_oj0w)

SONG LIST

- My Heavenly Father Loves Me (228)
- Choose the Right Way (160)
- When I Am Baptized (103)
- The Nativity Song (52)

GOSPEL ART BOOK

66 "The Second Coming"

Week 1:
I Remember Jesus When
I Take the Sacrament

SCRIPTURE

Luke 22:19

TALK

The star on a Christmas tree is a symbol. When you see a symbol, it helps you to remember something else. In our church, we use symbols like the Christmas star all year long. We can find symbols at the temple, in the songs we sing, and in the scriptures.

The sacrament is one of those symbols. The bread and water help us remember Jesus's body and His blood. Jesus sacrificed His body and blood for us when He died. When we take the sacrament, we promise to remember Jesus always. Next time you take the sacrament, watch and listen closely. Look for symbols that teach you about Jesus and how He died for you. Your parents and the Holy Ghost can help you find symbols. It's also important to be reverent during the sacrament. When you are reverent, the people around you can find symbols too, and you can all remember Jesus together.

LESSON

Discussion: Ask the children if they know why we celebrate Christmas. Explain that we celebrate Jesus's birth because He was our Savior. This means that He atoned for each of us so we can return to live with Heavenly Father. When we take the sacrament, we remember the sacrifice Jesus made. Each week when we take the sacrament, we can focus on and remember Jesus, just like we focus on and remember Him at Christmastime.

97

Activity: Help the children to make sacrament books that they can look at each week during the sacrament. Display several pictures of Christ around the room. (See the table below for suggested pictures from the *Gospel Art Book*.) Have the children fold two pieces of paper in half. Use a stapler to attach the papers and form a spine for the book. Then have the children draw pictures of scenes from Christ's life on each page of their books.

SUGGESTED PICTURES

32	Simeon Reverencing the Christ Child
34	Boy Jesus in the Temple
40	Jesus Calms the Storm
49	Jesus Raising Lazarus from the Dead
54	The Last Supper
56	Jesus Praying in Gethsemane
59	Mary and the Resurrected Jesus Christ

Application and Review: Ask the children if they have ever wished that we could celebrate Christmas all year. Point out that part of celebrating Christmas is thinking about Christ, and we can do that each week when we take the sacrament. Encourage the children to remember Christ and His atoning sacrifice as they take the sacrament each week.

Week 2:
I Remember Jesus to Help Me Make Good Choices

SCRIPTURE

Alma 37:47

TALK

Jasmine loves to do puzzles. She can do really hard ones with hundreds of pieces. One thing Jasmine has learned is that while she's working on a puzzle, she needs to look at the picture of what the puzzle will look like when it's finished. Looking at the finished picture helps Jasmine figure out which pieces to work on first and where they might go.

If you think about it, Jesus is like a finished puzzle picture. He lived a perfect life. When we look at His life and His example, we can figure out how to live a perfect life too. Whenever you need to make a choice, it's like you're holding a puzzle piece. You could try to figure out what to choose on your own, but that would be like trying to do a puzzle without looking at the picture. None of us can become perfect without Jesus. But if you follow His example and try your best, He will help you with all your choices so that someday you can become just like Him.

LESSON

Discussion: Show the children "Moses and the Brass Serpent" (GAB, 16) and explain that the brass serpent in this story represents Jesus Christ. All the Israelites needed to do was look at the serpent, and they would be healed. In the same way, our spirits can be healed when we look to Jesus for help. Jesus was a perfect example for us. Whenever we need to make a choice, we can think about what Jesus would do, and then we can follow His example.

Activity: Tell a "popcorn" story. To do this, you or another leader can begin the story. Be sure to include a choice that someone in the story has to make. If the person in the story chooses to follow what Jesus would choose, move a dot up on the board. If the person in the story chooses something Jesus would not choose, move the dot down. After a couple of choices, say, "Popcorn, _____," and fill in the blank with the name of someone who wants to continue telling the story. Ask the children to raise their hands if they want to help tell the story. Young children may need some help with this activity, but they can still participate with some coaching. As a group, see if you can get the dot to reach the top of the board. Depending on how much time you have and how the story goes, you can keep the first story going, or you can end it and start a new story one instead. If you're having trouble thinking of a story to tell, you can use a story from the scriptures, such as Lehi's family traveling through the wilderness or the story of Jonah.

Application and Review: Remind the children that they can always look to Jesus for an example, just like the Israelites looked at the brass serpent. The Holy Ghost will help us to know how Jesus would act in any situation. Encourage them to always follow Jesus so they can make good choices that will lead them back to Heavenly Father.

Week 3:
Jesus Was Born as God's Son on Earth

SCRIPTURE

Isaiah 9:6

TALK

So many people were excited for Jesus to be born. They had looked forward to it for a long time. They wanted to meet their King. But some people were hoping Jesus would make a big entrance. They did not expect Him to be born as a little baby in a stable.

Jesus and Heavenly Father knew what would be best. Heavenly Father often uses small and simple things to make great big things happen. When Jesus was born, it seemed like a small thing. But in fact, it was the beginning of a great big thing that would change the whole world forever.

Sometimes you might feel small. You might think the things you do don't matter or make a difference, but it's important to remember that Jesus was once small too. Jesus and Heavenly Father love you. They care about all the big and small things you do. As you make small good choices, you can change your life in big ways.

LESSON

Discussion: Ask the children to name some people who got to see Jesus soon after He was born. Their answers might include Mary, Joseph, the shepherds, the wise men, and Anna and Simeon. Discuss how each of these people might have felt and how the Spirit helped them to know who Jesus was and what He would do for us.

Activity: Watch Glad Tidings of Great Joy: The Birth of Jesus Christ (Mormon Channel, https://www.youtube.com/watch?v=x CxV9CbC180&t=1s)

Application and Review: Explain that just as each person who witnessed Christ as a baby needed to use the Spirit to know who He would become, we also need to use the Spirit to gain a testimony of Jesus. Encourage the children to learn more about Jesus and strengthen their testimonies of Him at Christmastime and all year long.

Week 4:
Someday Jesus Will Come
to the Earth Again

SCRIPTURE

Matthew 24:30–31

TALK

John was one of Jesus's good friends. He was also an Apostle. Because he was righteous, John learned many things from Jesus and from the Holy Ghost. He wrote down what he learned. Later John's writings became part of the New Testament. One of the books John wrote is called Revelation. This book tells us what will happen when Jesus comes again.

John wrote about many signs and wonders that would come before Jesus returned. Some of those signs are already happening. It's exciting to think that Jesus will come back to the earth someday. We can get ready for His return by sharing the gospel with our friends and neighbors. And we can be sure to make good choices so that when Jesus comes, He will be happy to see us and we will be happy to see Him. Reading the scriptures, especially books like Revelation, will help us prepare for the day when Jesus will return.

LESSON

Discussion: Tell the children the story of the ten virgins in your own words. (See Matthew 25:1–13.) Explain how this story teaches us that we need to prepare for Jesus's Second Coming. Ask the children to name some things we can do to prepare to see Jesus again. Point out that we do not know when Jesus will return, but we do know that we will see Him again someday and that we should prepare now so that when He does come, we are ready to be with Him and return to our Heavenly Father.

Activity: Sing "I Wonder When He Comes Again" (82). At the end of each line, invite one child to stand and share something we can do to prepare for the Second Coming.

Application and Review: Encourage the children to prepare to be with Jesus again by practicing gospel habits now. This will help them to store oil in their lamps like the ten virgins in the story. Some of these gospel habits include reading the scriptures, saying prayers, keeping the sabbath day holy, and obeying and honoring parents. Invite the children to choose a gospel habit they want to improve and set a goal to do better at it in the coming year. Share your testimony that the Savior will return someday and that He wants each of us to be ready to live with Him and our Heavenly Father again.

Primary Program

The annual Primary sacrament meeting presentation is an opportunity for the children in Primary to share what they have been learning with the rest of the ward. Elaborate visuals, costumes, or videos are not appropriate for sacrament meeting. Focus instead on bringing the Spirit with music and simple testimonies. Try to keep your expectations age appropriate. Younger children may only be able to memorize a short line. On the other hand, you can keep older children engaged by asking them to perform some of the songs in small groups or to give longer talks. Organizing the children by their classes could help them to know when it will be their turn to speak.

This chapter begins with some general tips and ideas for preparing and giving your program. After this section you'll find a sample outline for the program that you can adapt to the needs of your children.

LEARNING THE SONGS FOR YOUR PRESENTATION

Music is a key part of your presentation and can help each child participate more actively. Help the children learn these six suggested songs by practicing them in different ways throughout the year.

He Sent His Son

Use the question-and-answer format of this song to help you practice it. Divide the children into two groups, and have one group sing the questions and the other group sing the answers. You might start by dividing the children according to gender or where they are sitting in the room. Then you could divide them by their birth months, the first letters of their names, their favorite colors, and so forth. Repeating the song several times will help the children learn all the lyrics.

I Will Follow God's Plan

This song repeats the words "my," "me," and "I" several times in its lyrics. Have the children help you think of an action to do each time you sing one of these words. For example, you could raise your hands or stand up. When you practice this song, have two or more children come to the front of the room and perform the action while you all sing. Then ask the children in front to choose a new action and trade places with some of the children who are sitting down.

Behold the Great Redeemer Die

Since this is a sacrament hymn, we sing it fairly often, and the tune may be familiar to the children, even if the words are not. As you teach them each verse, be sure to talk about what the lyrics mean and explain any words they may not know. You might consider creating word strips or flashcards of any unfamiliar words and passing them out to older children so they can read the words and their definitions to the group. When you sing one of the words, have the child holding that word stand and raise the word up high for everyone to see.

Families Can Be Together Forever

The rhythm in this song varies. In some places it moves quickly, and in other places it is slow and thoughtful. Start by first teaching the children to clap along with the accompaniment. Then have them fill in words while they clap, and finally sing the words without clapping. It may be helpful to learn the chorus first and then each verse.

Baptism

The melody in this song contains some interesting intervals. Try having the children hum along with the music first while you move your hand up and down to show the children whether to sing higher or lower. As you learn each verse, explain the different parts of the story. The first verse sets the scene and gives the basic action. The second verse includes some dialogue between Jesus and John the Baptist. And the third verse gives an explanation for us of the lesson we should learn from the story. Talk about what it means to be baptized by immersion, and be sure to ask the children if they have any additional questions about the lyrics.

Search, Ponder, and Pray

You can use simple actions to help the children remember the lyrics in each line of this song. Teach the children each action, and then practice doing them together while you listen to the music. Use the actions in the table below or make up your own.

WORDS	ACTION
I	Point to Self
Love	Cross arms over chest
Read the Scriptures	Place hands together and open like a book
Heart	Place hand on chest
Search	Shade eyes with one hand and look around room
Ponder	Place one finger on forehead
Pray	Fold arms and bow head
Understand	Place a finger from each hand on temples

Preparing for Your Presentation

In addition to having the children practice the songs and their individual speaking parts, you will want to have them practice reverence on the stand, how to conduct themselves during the meeting, and how to speak into the microphone correctly. To this end, you may want to plan to have the Primary give a special musical number in sacrament meeting in August or even July. This will give you a chance to teach the children how to reverently walk to the front of the chapel, assemble themselves to sing, and project their voices. You could also introduce a microphone in one of your practices and have the children who participate in the lesson that day use it to answer questions or read scriptures. You may want to come up with a simple hand symbol for reverence that you use in your Primary. Make sure the children know what it is and what it means so that you can use it to signal to them nonverbally during the Primary presentation and during your practices.

Practices for the presentation should not take away unnecessarily from family time. If you have a large Primary, you might consider breaking your practices into sessions for junior and senior Primary to help you use your practice time more efficiently. You might also think about providing coloring pages or some other quiet activity for younger children to keep them occupied while the older ones are practicing their parts. In general, it is best to practice special musical numbers, like those performed by only one child or one class, separately so as not to waste time with the larger group.

If you plan to have the children sit on the stand for the entire meeting, you will want to plan a seating arrangement that ensures reverence. If necessary, separate children who cannot sit next to each other without distracting others. Be strategic in where you place teachers.

Have the children practice standing and making their way to the microphone reverently. If possible, give the children their parts as early as possible so that they have time to learn them before the presentation. Don't worry about perfection as you're practicing, and avoid stopping to fix little things. The point is to help the children get used to the overall flow of the presentation.

SAMPLE PRESENTATION IDEAS

It's a good idea to begin the presentation with a short introduction from a member of the Primary presidency. You could say something like:

> This year in Primary we are learning to follow the Savior. We know that through His plan, we can live with our families forever. Each month we have learned how we can follow God's plan as a family so that we can live together eternally. Some of the specific topics we have learned about include following the examples and teachings of Jesus and ancient and modern prophets. We know they set good examples that will help us follow this plan with our families. We have also learned about some gospel habits we can begin while we are young that will help us to progress on our way back to Heavenly Father. These include things like praying in faith, studying the scriptures, keeping the sabbath day holy, and obeying and honoring our parents. Today we are excited to present what we have learned about these topics with you. We know Heavenly Father loves each one of us. That is why He gave us our families. We love Him too, and we love the people in our families. We want to live with them forever, as part of Heavenly Father's great plan of happiness.

You may want to have an older child or group of older children act as narrators throughout the program, introducing each new monthly topic. Alternatively, you could ask one of the teachers or leaders to fill this role. The remainder of this sample outline will follow this structure:

Topic: Simple introduction that could be given by a teacher or narrator.

- Sample line for young children
- Sample part for older children

- Idea for a talk from one older child

You do not need to include both older and younger children for each topic. Use the Spirit to help you create a structure and presentation that works for the children in your Primary. Try to leave time at the end of your program for a member of the bishopric to offer some brief remarks.

SAMPLE OUTLINE

Introduction from Primary presidency. (See above.)

Song: "He Sent His Son"

Heavenly Father's Plan: Heavenly Father presented a plan before we were born. We chose to follow this plan so we could come to Earth and live in a family. We knew that being part of a family would help us to learn and grow.

- Heavenly Father gave me a family.
- Families are an important part of Heavenly Father's plan. He wanted each of us to come to Earth and learn to make good choices. He gave us our families so we would have people to love and teach us while we are here on the earth.
- You could have one of the older children give an overview of the plan of salvation or talk about what we need to do in order to have an eternal family. Have the child share his or her testimony of these doctrines and express gratitude for this plan and for families.

Song: "I Will Follow God's Plan"

Following the Plan: Part of Heavenly Father's plan included creating the earth as a place for us to live with our families. He also gave us many things to help us return to Him. He gave us a Savior, Jesus Christ, to set an example for us and atone for our sins and mistakes. He also gave us our bodies and the gift of agency so we can make our own choice to follow His plan.

- I am grateful for the Earth and for my body.
- Agency is the ability to choose for ourselves. I can choose to follow the example that Jesus Christ set for me. When I make a mistake, I know I can repent and continue to follow Heavenly Father's plan.
- Have one of the older children talk about how our bodies are created in the image of God. Ask the child to share some ways we can take good care of our bodies and how they are temples for our spirits.

Jesus Atoned for Us: Because He loved us, Jesus volunteered to come to Earth to teach us how to live righteously. He lived a perfect life, and then He died to save us from our sins, our mistakes, and all of the other bad things that happen in our fallen world.

- Jesus died so that I could return to Heavenly Father.
- I know that Jesus loves me, and I want to follow His example. I have faith in His mercy and atoning power. I know that if I repent, He will forgive me and help me to become better.
- Ask an older child to share the story of Jesus's death and Resurrection, including His appearance to the Nephites. Have the child focus on how Jesus overcame death so that we could live again.

Song: "Behold the Great Redeemer Die"

My Family: Families are central to Heavenly Father's plan. He wanted us to be part of a family so we could learn to become more like Him. We know that each member of a family has a special role to fulfill.

- I can help my family by listening to my parents.
- Families are so important in our church because everything the gospel teaches us is to help us live with our families forever. We know that if we are righteous, each of us can enjoy the blessings of an eternal family.

- Assign an older child to speak on what the family proclamation teaches us about the roles of mothers and fathers.
Encourage the child to share examples of how his or her
own parents fulfill these roles.

Song: "Families Can Be Together Forever"

Following the Prophet: Prophets have always been part of Jesus's true church. They can receive revelation from Heavenly Father to lead our whole church. We are blessed to have a prophet in our day who helps us to know what we should do.

- The prophet teaches us what Heavenly Father wants us to know.
- I can learn from the prophets in the scriptures. They wrote down their words for us so we could read them today. My favorite scripture prophet is _____ because he taught us to _____. (Help the child fill in the blanks in this sentence with his or her favorite scripture prophet and one of that prophet's teachings.)
- You could have one of the older children talk about listen-ing to the prophet during general conference. Have the child discuss some of the things the prophet has told us to do recently and why it is important to have a prophet in our day.

Priesthood and Temples: We know that the priesthood is the power of God on the earth. One of the reasons Heavenly Father has given us this power is so that we can perform sacred ordinances in the temple that will seal our families eternally.

- The priesthood blesses my family through sacred ordinances.
- I am learning how to do family history work so that I can help the people in my family who died before I was born. I can use the computer to learn more about them and to

make sure they have the chance to receive the blessings of the temple.

- Ask one of the older children in your Primary to share how he or she is preparing to go to the temple to do baptisms for the dead.

Baptism: When we choose to be baptized, we are following the example Jesus set for us. Baptism is a covenant that we make with our Heavenly Father. It allows us to receive the gift of the Holy Ghost to guide us every day.

- Someday I want to be baptized like Jesus was.
- When I was baptized, I felt _____. I knew that Heavenly Father wanted me to be baptized so that I could return to live with Him. I am grateful to have the Holy Ghost as a companion, comforter, and guide in my life.
- Invite an older child to speak on the symbols of baptism and how they relate to Jesus Christ's Atonement and Resurrection. Have the child share how taking the sacrament is a time to renew all our covenants, including the covenant we made when we were baptized.

Song: "Baptism"

Family Learning and Fun: Wholesome activities help our families to grow in love and in the gospel. When we pray, read the scriptures, have family home evening together, and keep the sabbath day holy, our homes become sacred places where we can feel the Spirit.

- My family can live the gospel by studying the scriptures together.
- I love family home evenings. It is a special time when we can grow stronger as a family and learn the gospel together. One of our favorite things to do as a family for family home evening is _____.

- Ask an older child to speak on the importance of keeping the sabbath day holy. Have the child share what he or she does on the sabbath to make it a special day to worship God.

Living the Gospel: In our families, we learn how to live the gospel. We learn things like being honest, serving others, and being grateful. When we live the gospel well, we can set a good example for our friends and the other people in our families.

- When I serve others, I am serving God.
- I am learning to be grateful every day. I try to notice the blessings Heavenly Father has given me so I can remember to thank Him in my prayers. When I am grateful, I don't worry as much about what I don't have because I can see how much He has already given me.
- You could have one of the older children talk about how he or she is trying to set a good example of living the gospel for the younger children in Primary. Ask the child to discuss why it is important to set a good example and how our actions can influence the people around us.

Song: "Search, Ponder, and Pray"

The Family Proclamation: We know that the family proclamation was revealed to modern prophets and apostles for our day. We are grateful for what it teaches us about families and how important they are.

- My family can be happy when we do what Jesus taught.
- The family proclamation teaches us that marriage is an essential part of Heavenly Father's plan. I am preparing now to enter the temple someday so I can be married in the temple. I know that when we are married in the temple, we are sealed as a family forever.
- Ask an older child to study the family proclamation and share a brief testimony about it. You might suggest that

the child memorize a portion of the proclamation and recite it as part of his or her talk.

Gospel Habits: Faith, prayer, repentance, and forgiveness are all important parts of living the gospel. We can establish these gospel habits while we are young so that they become natural parts of our own lives and by extension natural parts of our families.

- Having faith means believing in things we can't see.
- I know that I can repent whenever I make a mistake. Because Jesus has forgiven me, I do not have to focus on my sins or mistakes. Instead I can keep trying to become better. Repentance helps me move forward on my journey back to Heavenly Father.
- You could have one of the older children talk about a time when he or she needed to forgive someone. Encourage the child to share what it felt like to forgive and how forgiving others helps us to feel better.

Worshipping Jesus: The scriptures teach us that Jesus descended below all things so that He would know how to take care of us. As part of this, He was born in a lowly stable and He suffered on the cross. We know He loves each of us, and we love Him too.

- Jesus was born on the earth, and someday He will return again.
- Many people thought Jesus would be born as a great king or ruler. But instead He was a humble carpenter and teacher. He taught us how to love one another and love and serve God. I am grateful for His example.
- Invite an older child to share his or her testimony of the Savior. Have the child talk about how learning more about Jesus helps him or her to become more like Him.

Closing remarks from a member of the bishopric.

ADDITIONAL IDEAS

ADDITIONAL IDEAS

ADDITIONAL IDEAS

ADDITIONAL IDEAS

About the Author

Heidi Doxey is the author of eight previous volumes in the Tiny Talks and Time to Share series, one novel, and three board books: *1, 2, 3 with Nephi and Me!* and *Jesus Was Just like Me*, and *I Am Grateful for Colors* (forthcoming 2019).

Heidi currently lives in a tiny house in Northern California and works as a content editor for a software company. When she's not writing, she loves to read, go hiking, and spend time with her family.

Scan to visit

www.girlwithalltheanswers.blogspot.com